A SCENTED PALACE

A SCENTED PALACE

The Secret History of Marie Antoinette's Perfumer

Elisabeth de Feydeau

translated by Jane Lizop

I.B. TAURIS

LONDON · NEW YORK

Published in 2006 by I.B.Tauris & Co. Ltd
6 Salem Road, London W2 4BU
175 Fifth Avenue, New York, NY 10010
www.ibtauris.com

In the United States of America and Canada distributed by Palgrave
Macmillan, a division of St Martin's Press, 175 Fifth Avenue, New York,
NY 10010

ISBN 10: 1 84511 189 3
ISBN 13: 978 1 84511 189 2

A full CIP record for this book is available from the British Library
A full CIP record for this book is available from the Library of
Congress

Library of Congress catalog card: available

Typeset in Palatino Linotype by A. & D. Worthington, Newmarket
Printed and bound in Great Britain by
TJ International Ltd, Padstow, Cornwall

Contents

To Guillaume,
To Charles, Aliénor and Cordélia

Introduction

The events of the French Revolution remain some of the most vivid and compelling in the whole of European history. They constituted the point at which the Europe of the *ancien régime*, dominated by absolute monarchs, ended and a new era began, an era in which power came to be vested in the people of the continent. At the time of the Revolution, the reaction in Europe was intense. The initial sympathy that many felt for the revolutionaries faded as the revolutionary regime became increasingly violent – a reaction perhaps typified by Edmund Burke's famous *Reflections on the Revolution in France*, a classic work of English conservatism. Those who continued to feel sympathy for the revolutionaries may be represented by Thomas Paine, whose famous work *The Rights of Man* was written in response to Burke's *Reflections*. The deaths of the King and Queen of France, Louis XVI and Marie Antoinette, reverberated throughout Europe and continue to inspire sympathy and provoke debate. The enduring images of the French Revolution – the guillotine, the sans culottes, trico-teuses – have had a lasting impact on European culture and literature: Charles Dickens's *A Tale of Two Cities* and Victor Hugo's *Les Misérables* are perhaps the most familiar examples of the latter, while the ideas of the French philosophers and revolutionaries influenced many developments in politics throughout the nineteenth century, and beyond.

The papers of Jean-Louis Fargeon provide us with a new perspective on the events of the revolutionary years. This is the story of the life of a member of the bourgeoisie, a skilled perfumer and tradesman, whose position as a supplier of luxury commodities to the French Court at Versailles gave him a singular experience of the Revolution. It illustrates how even a man with republican beliefs, engendered by his readings of Enlightenment philosophy, could have those beliefs undermined by his experience of the violent spiral of events during the Revolution.

Jean-Louis Fargeon's story touches on many aspects of life in eighteenth-century France, in particular the development of a bourgeois family and career, and the social mores of the bourgeoisie. Descriptions of Parisian society and commerce provide a window into the ways of life of the time, especially into the culture of commerce and shopping. Through Fargeon's relations with the royal Court, we gain privileged access to the world of Marie Antoinette, the most famous of French queens, and a fascinating perspective on her life. The book recounts details of Court etiquette and ceremony, but most particularly deals with Marie Antoinette's fascination with dress and fashions – a fascination which was to contribute to her downfall. We learn details of the extravagant creations of Marie Antoinette's favourite milliner and dressmaker, Rose Bertin, and hairdresser, Léonard, and, of course, of the perfumes and cosmetics created for the Queen by Jean-Louis Fargeon. The luxury goods market in Paris was vibrant; the consumption of such items was essential for aristocrats.

The accounts of these products include fascinating information on the development of the cosmetics and perfume industry and its relation to scientific developments. These in turn were related to the Enlightenment, the great intellectual movement of the eighteenth century, which was embodied in the works of philosophers such as Diderot, Condorcet, Rousseau and Voltaire. These *philosophes* discussed ideals of freedom, equality and the rights of man, which had a profound effect on many members of the French middling classes, including Fargeon. Such ideas were promoted by France's involvement in the American War of Independence; the new American republic showed that Enlightenment ideals could be put into actual political practice.

The example of the American Revolution was an important element in creating the political climate necessary for revolution in France. Eighteenth-century or *ancien régime* France was governed by the system known as absolutism, in which all power was concentrated in the figure of the monarch. The system had been developed in its full form by the most famous of French monarchs, Louis XIV, the Sun King. His descendants, Louis XV (reigned 1714–1774) and Louis XVI (1774–1792), were less successful. Louis XV's scandalous private life and mismanagement of finances had left him deeply unpopular by the time of his death; although Louis XVI and Marie Antoinette were initially received with enthusiasm, the problems were not resolved during their reign. Indeed, Louis XVI's decision to provide military aid to the American revolutionaries during the War of Independence only deepened the financial woes of the state. The soldiers' contacts with the American revolutionaries further served to spread radical ideas. The bourgeoisie was the most heavily taxed section of the population and its members resented the fact that they had no power, in contrast to the privileged nobility and clergy – echoing the feelings expressed in the American cry, 'no taxation without representation'. The system of government in France seemed archaic and unjust in comparison to the American example and the ideals developed in the works of the *philosophes*. The popularity of the King and Queen plummeted, with libellous and pornographic pamphlets circulating widely in Paris. They accused Marie Antoinette of affairs with men and women from her close circle, or *société*, and equated this private debauchery with her supposed policy of influencing politics in favour of Austria, her own country.

It was not only the bourgeoisie who were unhappy with the government of Louis XVI and his ministers. The minister of finances, Calonne, convened an Assembly of Notables in

1787 in order to promote a plan to reform the financial situation. However, the Notables were so appalled by the level of the financial deficit that they forced Louis to dismiss Calonne, and the plan fell by the wayside. This marked the first point at which the control of royal authority over government was challenged. Gradually, over the next two years, it became further and further endangered, as the King's ministers tried to pass reforming measures in the face of a distrustful populace and institutions that had lost faith in monarchical authority. The provincial courts or *parlements*, shocked by the scale of mismanagement, refused to pass reforming measures and their members began to petition for a meeting of the Estates General, the parliamentary body of France, which had not met since 1614. Louis was forced to accede to these demands, and the Estates General met in the spring of 1789. Royal authority was therefore no longer paramount, and France was *en route* to becoming a constitutional monarchy.

The new Estates General had caused problems even before the deputies gathered on 5 May 1789. The 1614 Estates General had been composed of representatives of the three estates (the clergy, the nobility and the people) in roughly equal numbers. However, in 1789 the Third Estate had demanded double the number of deputies, to match the greater tax contribution made by the bourgeoisie. Louis XVI and his ministers wanted to proceed directly to dealing with the financial problems; but as soon as the Estates met, disputes arose over whether the deputies should vote by estate or by head – the Third Estate, naturally, wished to vote by head, while the more traditionally minded members of the First and Second Estates wished to preserve their influence by voting by estate. On 17 June the Third Estate declared the principle that national sovereignty is vested in the nation; its deputies then declared that they now convened as the National Assembly, a body representing the people. Louis XVI himself may not have been totally averse to some forms of reform, but many of his courtiers, especially the royal princes, were determined to uphold the position of the monarchy, and they had considerable influence with the King and Queen. Louis therefore attempted to subdue the Assembly, shutting down its halls. The deputies reacted by reconvening in the royal tennis court and swearing an oath not to disband until a new constitution had been created; this was the famous Tennis Court Oath of 20 June 1789. Louis attempted to promote a compromise but failed, and was forced to order the remaining deputies to join the National Assembly. On 9 July the body was renamed the National Constituent Assembly.

At the same time, the city of Paris was experiencing considerable upheaval. The surrounding countryside had suffered several years of poor harvests in the 1780s, and Paris was full of hungry, disaffected people. By early July 1789 the city was on the brink of revolt, and the citizens had formed a revolutionary Commune. When news reached the citizens on 12 July that Louis had dismissed his chief minister, the popular Necker, the people began to gather at the Hotel de Ville, in the belief that a conservative coup was about to occur. On 14 July the crowd proceeded to the Bastille prison, where they demanded the release of the arms and ammunition held there. Eventually the insurgents stormed the prison and liberated it, releasing seven prisoners held there and killing the governor.

Following the storming of the Bastille, the National Constituent Assembly became the governing body of the country; the deputies set about dismantling the old feudal structures, and on 24 August issued the Declaration of the Rights of Man and of the Citizen, which promulgated popular sovereignty and equality of rights and opportunity. The Assembly also consolidated the public debt, thereby restoring public confidence and the credit of the government, and created a committee of subsistence to deal with food shortages. Most significantly for the monarchy, the Assembly vested all powers in itself and allowed the King a suspensive veto only. France had effectively become a constitutional monarchy. Louis XVI began to gather troops around him at Versailles, but his actions only served to alienate his subjects still further, and to promote insurrection in Paris. On 5 October the Parisian mob marched to Versailles, where they murdered Marie Antoinette's guards and broke into her apartments. Marie Antoinette, well aware that she was the most unpopular member of the royal family, was forced to appear alone before the crowd; but, impressed by her bravery, they did not harm her. Nonetheless the royal family were forced to return with the crowd to Paris, where they were installed in the old and dilapidated palace of the Tuileries under the supervision of the National Guard. Here they were effectively house prisoners, unable to leave the city. Although Marie Antoinette tried to ignore the public hatred directed towards her, she was affected; she had to attend her daughter's first communion in disguise.

Over the next months, the Constituent Assembly continued with its work of forming a new constitution. Among other measures, it began to attack the privileges of the clergy, abolishing tithes, confiscating and monetizing church lands, and eventually producing the Civil Constitution of the Clergy, under which the clerics became employees of the state and swore allegiance to the constitution. The Constituent Assembly also abolished all noble titles and orders of knighthood, along with hereditary offices, thereby further dismantling the apparatus of the *ancien régime*. Louis XVI was forced reluctantly to accede to these measures. Meanwhile, the Assembly attacked other structures of privilege further down the social order, affecting members of the bourgeoisie such as Jean-Louis Fargeon: the d'Allarde Law of 2 March 1791 abolished guilds and masterships, thereby allowing any individual to buy a licence to practise a trade. However, the Le Chapelier Law of June 1791 showed that the revolutionary work of the Constituent Assembly was largely the work of the middle classes: it banned workers' organizations and strikes.

It became increasingly clear that the royal family were in an untenable position: they were not even allowed to visit the royal palace at Saint Cloud to take communion during Holy Week, and the King's position was ever more circumscribed. They began to make plans to escape Paris, intending to flee to Montmédy, the encampment of their supporter General de Bouillé, where they would be able to make contact with émigrés and other supporters abroad. However, their preparations were so extensive, and they themselves were so unrealistic and naïve (as exemplified by the construction of the enormous travelling berlin, and Marie Antoinette's insistence on taking her vast toilet kit) that it is perhaps unsurprising that they were apprehended at Varennes. They were forced to return to the Tuileries and Louis XVI was left as a figurehead, although he did retain his suspensive veto. Despite this, he was still able to accept the Constitution of 1791, an action which received much public approval. The Constituent Assembly was then able to cease sitting, and was replaced by the Legislative Assembly on 1 October 1791.

The course of the French Revolution was influenced to a considerable degree by the threat other European powers posed to the new system. An alliance between the Empire and Prussia, aided by French émigrés including the King's brother, the Comte d'Artois, had been formed to oppose the revolutionaries. The Pillnitz Declaration of 27 August 1791, which asked that the monarchs of Europe should join together to ensure the liberty of the French King and Queen and the monarchical settlement of France, actually made matters much worse for the royal family. The threat to the Revolution merely made the citizenry more defiant, and the situation in Paris grew increasingly tense. Louis found it impossible to form a ministry that could find accommodation with the republican left. The French Revolutionary Wars began in April 1792, with a disastrous French campaign in the Austrian Netherlands. The army was in confusion, discipline was poor and morale was low: the threat of an invasion increased, and with it the insurrectionary atmosphere. On 9 July 1792 a new revolutionary Commune swept to power in Paris, dominated by the revolutionary lawyer and republican Georges Jacques Danton.

The state of affairs brought about by the Revolutionary Wars was only exacerbated by the Manifesto, issued on 25 July 1792 by the Duke of Brunswick, commander of the Austro-Prussian army (then massing just outside the French borders),

which stated that if the least 'violence or outrage' was offered
to the royal family, the Austrian and Prussian armies would
subject Paris to martial law and destruction. On 20 June the
Parisians had invaded the Tuileries in arms; the Brunswick
Manifesto, issued at a time when members of the National
Guard were gathered in Paris for the Bastille anniversary
celebrations, inflamed public opinion and united Parisians
against the monarchy. On 10 August the royal family was once
again assailed in the Tuileries; the explicit aim of this second
invasion was to depose the King. Louis XVI, shaken by the
disloyalty of some of the National Guard regiments stationed
around the palace, decided to retreat to the halls of the Legislative Assembly. There the deputies acceded to the demands
of the insurrectionary Paris Commune by suspending the
King from all his functions and by dissolving the constitution in favour of a new National Convention, to be elected by
manhood suffrage. The royal family were incarcerated in the
Temple prison.

The revolutionary Paris Commune thus became the
real power behind government. Under the influence of the
Commune, the Legislative Assembly began to use the guillotine in August, executing political criminals. Thanks to
the Austro-Prussian army, which had invaded France on 19
August and which, by 2 September, stood at Verdun with the
way to Paris wide open, the Commune had begun imprison-
ing large numbers of suspected counter-revolutionaries. In
the panic inspired by news of the fall of Verdun on 2 September, groups of insurrectionary citizens went round the prisons, killing the inmates. Around 1,400 people died during the
five days of the prison terror, among them Marie Antoinette's
intimate friend, the Princesse de Lamballe, whose head was
paraded around the Temple prison on a pike in the hope
that the Queen would see it. The royal family's only hope
of survival lay with the invading army, but it never arrived.
It had met the French army at Valmy on 19 September, and
though the battle itself was indecisive, the failure of the Prussian troops to defeat the French signalled a turning-point in

the campaign. On 21 September, the day after it first convened, the National Convention declared the abolition of the monarchy and the beginning of the French Republic. On 3 December the Convention decided that Louis XVI should face trial on the basis of documents discovered in a secret cache at the Tuileries. He appeared before the Convention on 11 December, and again on the 26th, when he and his counsel mounted his defence. Despite their efforts, a majority of the Convention deputies found the King guilty of conspiring against liberty and the safety of the French state; there was a majority of only one for the punishment of unconditional death. Louis XVI seems to have expected to die. He was executed on 21 January 1793 at 10.22 a.m.

Despite the death of the monarch, the Revolution continued to develop. The National Convention saved France from invasion by the *levée en masse* or conscription and improved military discipline, and also put down insurrections and civil wars in France. The Constitution of 24 June 1793 was the first republican constitution. However, the government of the Convention was characterized by a series of exceptional measures, which displayed increasing radicalism and violence. On 10 March 1793 the Revolutionary Tribunal was set up to deal with political crimes; on 2 June of that year, there was a coup within the National Convention in favour of the hardline Jacobins, led by Danton. The Convention was also responsible for the Reign of Terror, stretching from September 1793 to July 1794, which was the chief cause of the ultimate downfall of the revolutionary Jacobin party, and of the revolutionary government itself. On 5 September the Convention institutionalized the Terror to repress internal enemies of France. Following this and the Law of Suspects, the Revolutionary Tribunal condemned thousands to death, including many revolutionaries. Marie Antoinette was among the first victims. On 2 August, suddenly and under cover of darkness, she had been moved to the Conciergerie prison – the prison that held those about to be condemned to death. Her health deteriorated rapidly. In mid-September she was placed in solitary confinement (it was on 17 September that the Law of Suspects authorized the charging of suspected counter-revolutionaries with 'crimes against liberty') and on 12 October she was summoned before the Revolutionary Tribunal for a preliminary examination; the trial itself was held on 14 October. The case against her was built on the evidence of witnesses, among them the radical revolutionary Hébert, who had coerced the Dauphin into signing a confession that his mother and aunt had sexually molested him. Despite a brave performance from Marie Antoinette, there was never any doubt that she would be sentenced to death. She was sent to the guillotine on the morning of 16 October. The only member of the immediate royal family to survive the Revolution was the Princess Marie-Thérèse, who died in exile in Austria in 1851.

The government of France moved towards that of a centralized and deeply repressive police state. No dissent from the party line of the Jacobins, then headed by the famous revolutionary Maximilien Robespierre, could be tolerated; as a result the extreme radicals such as Hébert were guillotined in the spring of 1794, closely followed by the more moderate wing headed by Danton. The work of the Revolutionary Tribunal was accelerated by the 'Loi du Grand Terreur' of 10 June 1794, which denied defendants any counsel and which decreed that execution was the only permissible punishment for those found guilty. The condemned were sent to the guillotine in batches, and at last Paris began to tire of the incessant bloodshed. Estimates of the total number of victims of the Terror range from 16,500 to 40,000. Robespierre, who had used the Terror to protect his own position, and who had instituted an unpopular state religion, the worship of the Supreme Being, eventually fell victim to his own tactics: a coup was staged on 17 July (9 Thermidor in the Revolutionary calendar), and the following day Robespierre and his supporters, including most of the revolutionary Paris Commune members, were executed.

The Thermidorian reaction, as it became known, was the end of the violent revolutionary period. A new form of government was instituted in September 1795, that of the Directory or Directoire, which consisted of two chambers and an executive of five Directors, elected from among the deputies. The new constitution guaranteed freedom of religion, of labour and of the press, but political societies and armed assemblies were expressly forbidden. The Convention had decreed that two-thirds of the Assembly deputies must be elected from the Convention deputies – a move designed to protect them from public disgust, which was so unpopular that it provoked an uprising in Paris. This was put down by a young general, Napoleon Bonaparte. The country continued to suffer from arbitrary government and the effects of foreign wars, and in 1799 Paris and other districts were once more on the verge of revolt. The Directors recalled Napoleon from his post in Egypt, and in a coup d'état on 9 November 1799 (18 Brumaire) he overturned the Directory and installed the Consulate. This consisted of three assemblies and an executive of three consuls; Napoleon as a matter of course became the pre-eminent consul, and functioned as an unacknowledged dictator. His popularity grew among many Frenchmen, as his promises of moderation and stability carried considerable appeal after the violence and upheaval of the revolutionary years; this was despite his use of many techniques of the *ancien régime*, which led the army and republicans to view him as a despot. France began to enjoy order and prosperity once again, and Paris was full of provisions and luxury commodities, destined for the houses and salons of the new elite. On 18 May 1804 the French Senate voted to declare Napoleon Emperor, and he crowned himself later that year. The Revolution was well and truly over.

Catherine Wright
Institute of Historical Research

Prologue

Tomorrow, on 9 Thermidor of Year II of the one and indivisible Republic, I, Jean-Louis Fargeon, perfume maker to the former royal court, will be tried before the Revolutionary Tribunal. My only desire is to clear myself of the crimes of which I am accused, crimes that I have never committed. Accusations that I am an enemy of liberty and a partisan of the old regime are untrue. While it is true that I hate the bloody chaos now called the Revolution, I remain a republican and faithful to the motto 'live free or die'.

By order of the Committee of Criminal Investigations, I have been held in this jail since 8 Nivôse, accused of being an enemy of the new order and of circulating counterfeit. My house at Chaumont, my former boutique in the rue du Roule, and my laboratory at Suresnes have all been placed under seal. My neighbours have denounced me. What sad times we live in, when men are led to accuse one another. The prisons are full. Trade has come to a standstill, and the work-shops are deserted. Too much innocent blood, too many intrigues and ambitions and too much treachery have blackened the face of the Revolution.

I am a man of science, a follower of progress. I concentrated my experiments, my knowledge and my inventions upon the subtle art of perfume. Paris has become the centre of science, of the arts and of taste. In the field of chemistry, a science that has witnessed so many discoveries in recent years, I have explored heretofore untrodden paths. In nature, I sought and found elements that could inspire the soul and evoke long-buried memories, and I used them in my creations. *What can one demand of my art today? To prove my patriotism, should I create a perfume based upon the odour of blood that permeates the air around the guillotine?*

As I languish in this fetid cell, sometimes the sweet scent of days gone by transports me to the salons and the gardens of a world where that rose among the lilies, the late Queen of France, blooms.

When the perfume of the past envelops me, my entire life falls into place, the way the compositions of my scents did. First the harmony of the main theme, before the dominant accents rush forth like a spring, wild, lively, as impatient as youth. And then, the touches from the heart throb sweet, accomplished and vibrant, like the fulfilment of a personality. And at last, heavy, persistent, tenacious, the basic tenor, the notes from deep down resonate, those that soared at the very beginning. Such was my art, and such was my life. Tomorrow I shall know if it must be taken from me.

I

The Main Theme
1748–1774

Olfaction is the sense of the imagination.
JEAN-JACQUES ROUSSEAU

❧ The scent of the garrigue ❧

Under the blinding sun, the streets and alleyways of Montpellier smell of citron and bergamot orange. The surrounding countryside is fragrant with the scent of thyme, wild thyme and lavender. Those who gather and distil the raw materials of perfume here make a good living. It is the ideal place for the birth of Jean-Louis Fargeon, future perfumer to the Queen of France and Navarre.

In the year of 1748, the Treaty of Aix-la-Chapelle ended the War of Austrian Succession in which France fought for the King of Prussia, and Louis XV was reigning over the most magnificent kingdom in the world. Montesquieu published *L'Esprit des lois*. The French drenched themselves in *eau admirable*, known today as eau de Cologne, after French soldiers brought it back from that city. A place in perfumery was Jean-Louis Fargeon's birthright, for the art had been a family tradition for over a century. As the first son, he received his father's Christian name when he was baptized, on 12 August at Notre-Dame des Tables.[1] One of his ancestors had been a wool merchant, and that ancestor's son, Jean, became prominent in 1655 as apothecary and perfumer to HRH Mademoiselle d'Orléans, his trademark being the 'Golden Vase'. His associates were Paul Portallès, master apothecary and perfumer, and

Jean Guiraud, master apothecary of Roquetaillade (Rouergue). Jean's children found other callings: one son became an adviser at the Court of Revenue, Aid and Finances, and another was Seigneur de la Lauze. Jean-Louis Fargeon descended from the branch of the youngest son, Claude Fargeon, whose offspring became perfumers to the Kingdom of France. One of them, his grandfather Antoine Fargeon, 'merchant perfumer', married Marie-Rose Roumieu on 27 January 1715 at Notre-Dame des Tables, and left her widowed in 1729. A strong woman, Marie-Rose took over and managed the business with the help of her nephew Antoine, who had spent fifteen months as an apprentice *garçon liquoriste* (a maker of liquors, distilled alcohols of fruit, flowers or plants). Jean-Louis Fargeon's maternal grandfather married Marguerite Salles on 21 January 1744, at Notre-Dame des Tables. Her sister Jeanne had married into one of the most important families of Montpellier's perfume industry, the Matte la Faveurs. Jean Jacques Joseph Mathieu Matte la Faveur had established his business in Grasse as perfume merchant and perfumer to the King.

It was said that the art of the perfumer had its origins in antiquity, but Jean-Louis Fargeon's father used to say that perfumery was born in Montpellier. The municipality supported this claim with the sort of gestures it made to honour visiting guests, and glass vials filled with scented water, powdered violets and other 'gifts of fragrance' replaced the traditional fruit preserves. The perfumer was part of a proud tradition that dated from the Middle Ages, when, according to the Provençal novel *Flamenca*, the fragrance of perfumes would waft through the streets of the town at Christmas time. The manuals of perfumery even referred to certain products as being *à la mode de Montpellier*, because they called for the addition of ingredients from the animal kingdom, such as civet or musk, to traditional recipes, to make their fragrances linger in a deeper, more bewitching way. Simon Barbe, Louis XIV's perfumer, referred thus in his formulae to *poudre de Cypre*, as made in Montpellier: 'Take two pounds of powder of pure oak moss which has been purged with flowers,' he instructed.

'Dissolve in it eighteen grains of civet, and a *demi-gros* of musk.'
He specified that the *toilette montpelliéraine* 'was enriched with
nine plants: iris, camanne root, rosewood, citrin-coloured
sandalwood, calamus, souchet, cinnamon, clove, ladanum, all
of which offer contrasting scents'.[2]

In France the first statutes concerning the profession had
been established in 1190 and constantly modified ever since.
The Fargeons' bible was the treatise by their ancestor, Jean,
'apothecary and perfumer of royal privilege'. In 1668 he had
perfected the recipes of a large number of products, classed
according to usage as either 'compositions for health' or
'perfumes for embellishment'. The work was a rich source
of formulae that had cemented the family's reputation. Various other treatises were considered authoritative references.
In Paris, using the pen name of Dejean, Antoine Hornot
published two major works propounding a theory of odours:
'that to which the nose is sensitive is composed of volatile
particles, subtle and penetrating, that not only touch the olfactory nerve, but spread throughout the entire brain.'[3] During
the same period, the German scientist von Haller published
an eight-volume anatomical and physiological encyclopaedia
which extensively explored the mechanism of breathing, a
prelude to understanding the olfactory phenomenon.

In Montpellier, a city known for its medical advances,
apothecaries had established their legal status in 1572, and
the independence of their corporation had been confirmed in
1674. They imported and manufactured drugs for patients and,
although they were not part of the merchant class, they were
authorized to sell perfumes. An apothecary would employ
about fifty vegetable and four or five animal substances in the
preparation of his products, and some of these were also used
in perfumery. The city's seaport was located at Aigues-Mortes,
but at the end of the previous century, Sète had superseded it
as the landing and unloading point for goods from the Orient,
much like Marseilles. Regional contacts with foreign countries
had furthered the progressive development of the business

of transforming scented raw materials. In 1669 one observer described Montpellier as a place where:

> Pharmacy and chemistry are at a high point of development, as is evident through the number of sharp professionals. The apothecaries' boutiques are beautiful and sweet smelling, full of syrups, and powder of Cyprus, liquors and perfumes for all kinds of grooming, sachets of scent and a thousand other things.[4]

Those who practised this business were known as *pébriers sobeyrans*, wholesalers, in contrast to *pébriers de mercat*, or retailers. The *especiayres* or *espiciers-apothicaires* prepared drugs for therapeutic use in particular, but it was acknowledged that they had learned the Arabian art of distilling essences and perfumes, an expertise which conferred upon them the title of *aromatarii*. This early stage of specialization was confirmed by a separation between the apothecaries and the spice and drug merchants, and the glove-makers-perfumers-distillers.

As descendants of the community of apothecaries, the Fargeons had reoriented the family business towards the art of the perfumer. All of the perfumers had their establishments in the same part of town, and they created strong family bonds among themselves through intermarriage. Their boutiques were all located in the busy streets of the western quarter, rues St Guilhem and de l'Aiguillerie, the Grand-Rue, the Faubourg de la Saunerie. The Fargeons established theirs in the Grand-Rue, across from the Traverse des Grenadiers. Jacques Matte La Faveur's shop was there too, opposite the Cheval Blanc.

Jean-Louis Fargeon was seven years old when Maria Antonia Josepha Joanna, Archduchess of Austria, who would later become Queen of France and his most illustrious client, was born on 2 November 1755. In the same year, a dreadful earthquake ravaged Lisbon, perhaps presaging the tragic destiny of the future Queen of France. The little boy from Montpellier, student at the parish school, was no doubt unaware of these events. He was learning reading, writing and in particular arithmetic, essential knowledge for a future merchant. He participated in small tasks and chores at the boutique, coddled in the gruff tenderness of his work-harried mother and father. The shop, facing the street, was his mother's domain, furnished with tables, sideboards and glass-windowed display cases. Ladders provided access to all kinds of containers: boxes of bergamot, cases of scent, snuffboxes made of horn, and an assortment of small bottles, vials, demijohns and jars full of essential oils of plants, known as *esprits*.

The boutique was redolent with the flowered notes of essences of rose, narcissus and orange blossom, and the perfume of citrus from Italy: lemon, orange, tangerine, citron, bergamot orange and grapefruit. Sandalwood and spice-smelling bark, cinnamon or *cascarille* added the exotic note of their Oriental origins, and an odour of resolutely medicinal camphor dominated all others and lent an unusual, tonic effect to the blend. Oils, powders and liquid scents smelled of rose, jasmine, violet, iris, daffodil, carnation and lavender as well as orange and lemon. Amber and orange blossom were quite popular, as well as musk, although in recent years customers had been less fond of the latter. Preparations most in demand were *poudre de mille fleurs, poudre d'ange* and *poudre de Chypre*, as well as *eaux à la Maréchale* or *eaux aux herbes de Montpellier*, toilet waters that smelled chiefly of thyme. There were also *eaux de propreté* (lotions for cleanliness), *eau de câpres* (made from the buds of the caper tree flower) and *vinaigres de toilette* (grooming vinegars), as well as bars of soap, creams and pomades.

The boutique also sold an assortment of small objects, displayed in appealing disarray[5]: bags for needlework, swan's down powder puffs, toothpicks, beauty spots, sponges, snuffboxes and tobacco pouches, even garters, and little baskets or sachets of perfumes. Gloves and mittens were also an important element of the stock for sale.[6] Along with perfume, some of their colleagues sold olives, anchovies in brine and brown sugar, but Fargeon's father frowned upon such additions, believing that they belonged at the grocer's. The 'second store', a term that referred to the back shop, contained large

receptacles and wooden boxes used for deliveries. There were
also baskets that served to present goods, once they had been
attractively decorated with cloth.

At the back of the room was the laboratory – the mysterious centre for the preparation of the boutique's specialities.
Here the perfumer reigned, amid his cauldrons and stills, his
presses, coils, skimmers and mortars. To the young Fargeon,
the casks that held the raw materials seemed gigantic. The
fragrance of all these perfumes, those of the nearby garrigue
and the more exotic scents that came from the Orient, made
him heady. All his life, he would treasure the memory of
these unusual blends, created with musk, amber, civet and
the resins of Arabia, incense, myrrh, opopanax gum resin and
galbanum.

Fargeon's grandmother, Marie-Rose, taught him nursery
rhymes and local legends, and sang him lullabies. He found
the tale of the *eau de la Reine de Hongrie* especially enchanting.
According to the legend, in the fourteenth century, the Queen
Jeanne, seventy-two years old, paralytic and gout-ridden, had
received a scented liquid from the hands of a hermit. It had
so charmed her that she rediscovered her strength and her
beauty, so much so that the King of Poland demanded her
hand in marriage when she was seventy-six. *Eau de la Reine
de Hongrie* was considered a panacea for maladies as diverse
as rheumatism, ringing in the ears, and stomach troubles,
and it was said to protect against epidemics. Above all, it was
known to revive a woman's youth and beauty. Perhaps it was
the image of the old woman, magically rendered desirable
by a perfume, that inspired the dream that Jean-Louis would
cherish from his early days to the end of his life: to make a
woman beautiful, to discover how to enhance the beauty of
her complexion, to conserve the freshness of her skin and to
hide its flaws, to change the colour of her hair and to make the
stains and marks of age disappear. For him, perfumery would
be closely linked to the art of cosmetics.

❧ A father who admired the philosophers ❦

Like so many bourgeois of the provinces, Jean-Louis Fargeon's father was fascinated by the ideas of the philosophers. He subscribed to the *Journal des savants* and to the *Avant-coureur*, a sheet published weekly that described the latest developments in the sciences, the liberal and mechanical arts, entertainment, industry and literature. Despite the considerable price, he had also subscribed to the *Dictionnaire Raisonné des sciences, des arts et des métiers* of Diderot and d'Alembert, better known as the *Encyclopédie*,[7] and he was furious to see his money returned in 1752, when the censors accused the works' authors of 'provocation against God and royal authority'.

Although the young Jean-Louis already possessed some of the rudiments of the trade, his father wanted him to have a solid academic background before embarking on his apprenticeship. With great foresight, Fargeon's father measured the advantages of the education of mind and body to a refined profession, one where the clientele would demand that one express oneself in proper language, not the Occitan dialect that was still commonly spoken in the provinces of the Midi of France. His wife had a more traditional vision of commerce.[8] The daughter of a fruit merchant, she thought the best kind of education was that gleaned at the vendor's stall and the cash drawer. The rule in the petit bourgeoisie of commerce was to take one's place by succeeding one's father, without cluttering the mind with useless knowledge. But, as Molière said, all power resides on 'the side that bears the beard', and so it was decided that the couple could make do without their son in the boutique while he studied the humanities at a school run by the Oratorian Order, in Montpellier.

On 29 July 1760 Jean-Louis Fargeon's father died, still young. The avid follower of the philosophers never lived to see the era of wisdom and virtue they foresaw. He left his widow with five children. She respected her late husband's wishes and engaged as chief assistant Jean Poncet from Sète, who would prove entirely capable, and left her eldest son, then twelve, with the Oratorians, where he continued his studies. He was a good student, perhaps not brilliant, but gifted with an exceptional memory with which he absorbed not only the teachings of his masters but the formulae of perfumery as well.

❧ The nose is the door to the soul ❦

Jean-Louis did not want to confine himself to perfume recipes. He wanted to understand the nature of the sense of smell. The Académie Française had summarily defined perfume as the agreeable smell exuded from something odorous, either by the application of fire or by some other means. An article from the *Encyclopédie* devoted to the perfumer described him as, 'both merchant and worker, who makes, sells, and uses all kinds of perfumes, hair powder, bars of soap, perfumed gloves, sachets of fragrance, pot-pourri, etc'.[9]

Jean-Louis Fargeon read the *Traité des sensations*, in which the philosopher Etienne Bonnot de Condillac exposed the educational role of the senses and told the parable of the statue whose creator had provided it with a nose as its only sense organ, since through smell alone the marble could acquire all other senses and claim complete access to the outside world. The statue, breathing in 'an odour of rose', had no actual image of the flower. 'It will be the odour of rose, of carnation, of jasmine, of violet, according to the objects that stimulate his organ. In a word, as far as he is concerned, odours are like modifications of himself or his ways of being.'[10]

Fargeon was inspired by this theory and by the philosophers who had rehabilitated and elevated the sense of smell. Diderot wrote, 'I found that, of all the senses, sight was the most superficial, hearing the most arrogant, smell the most voluptuous, taste the most superstitious and the least faithful, touch the most profound and the most philosophical.'[11] A revolution in chemistry was also at hand with the first experiments of Antoine Lavoisier, which the young man read about without yet really seizing their meaning. And an immense field was opening up in perfumery. Perfume was no longer simply the 'agreeable fragrance that pleases the sense of smell' mentioned in Savary's *Dictionnaire du commerce.*[12] It was a key to the soul. Fargeon became aware that he would be working for clients who were aesthetes, people who sought scents that were exquisite, subtle and new.

Each day, following his studies with Jean Poncet, Fargeon would plunge into the works of Voltaire he found in his father's library. He discovered Jean-Jacques Rousseau, the bard of nature and of sensitivity, whose lyric use of language spoke to him like a perfume that inspired and elevated the soul. Modern man, with his torments and his natural goodness, seemed to be born through Rousseau's pen. He had been the first to write that the man who feels surpasses the man who thinks, that the imagination 'broadens the scope of the possible' and dominates reason, which it can raise to the heights of the sublime. In *Les Rêveries du promeneur solitaire*, Rousseau asserted that the education of the senses was the essential and indispensable condition of successful overall education; in *L'Emile*, that odour, in particular the scent of others, was a powerful factor of attraction or repulsion through its action on the imagination. He told of his arrival in Paris, where he found himself indisposed by the nauseating effluvia of the Faubourg Saint Marcel. And he concluded that 'odours in and of themselves are weak sensations. They disturb the imagination more than meaning and affect not so much through what they emanate as what they inspire one to expect.' A new importance was accorded to the sense of smell, which was capable of evoking turbulent reactions in the soul, of resuscitating long-buried memories and of changing the mood of the moment. 'The real world has its limits, the world of the imagination is infinite; since we cannot expand one, let us shrink the other, for all the sorrows that make us unhappy are caused by the difference between them.'[13]

When she heard her son say that the nose was the door to the soul and that a philosopher was the source of this revelation, the widow Fargeon thought she was losing her mind but she was much reassured by the enthusiasm her son showed for developing his knowledge of the art of the perfumer as soon as he had finished school. The chief assistant from Sète continued the education Fargeon's father had begun a few years previously and assured his mother that her eldest son had a first-rate nose and was able to distinguish with little effort infinite fragrance notes.

Fargeon began to learn that most vegetable elements had a smell, sometimes pleasant, and that most flowers had the double advantage of pleasing both the eye and the sense of smell, but their fragrance disappeared with their fleeting beauty. The acidic saps, simple or in fermented form, gave off strong odours that were almost overwhelming because of their alkaline putrefaction. Heat or crushing extracted these fragrances, and the subtle matter contained in the essential oils of the plants was called *esprit*. For over a century, perfumers had known how to extract the *esprit recteur* by a process of maceration known as *enfleurage*. The technique was a speciality of Grasse and largely responsible for the little provincial town's prosperity, but it was also practised in Montpellier.

The apprentice had already expressed a preference for the natural. He distilled simple scented toilet waters, *esprits ardents*, and essential oils, and he learned to be wary of counterfeit substitutes for rare and costly substances. He gradually created his palette of perfume, some fragrances inspiring him more than others. He regularly sought ways to perfect the family preparations of cosmetics, rouges, make-up, soaps and creams to whiten the hands and the face, powders and opiate elixirs for the teeth, tablets and rinses to perfume the mouth. He created oils and various coloured powders, pomades and dyes for the hair, often wrestling with the problem of finding products that were effective but inoffensive. He was skilled in the traditional Montpellier speciality of making gloves that were dyed, then perfumed, *à la mode de Provence*, with certain flowers that were beneficial to the skin such as orange blossom, roses, nutmeg, tuberose and jasmine.

But despite all his efforts, the family business stagnated. The *liquoristes*, who claimed to be perfumers but really were not, were a source of unfair competition. Moreover, although many formulae were still characterized as '*à la mode de Montpellier*', the city was gradually losing ground to Grasse. Six Montpellier perfumers had had to declare bankruptcy since 1750, and the number of members of the corporation was decreasing. The community of perfumers of Grasse were the royal favourites, which benefited them greatly, whereas their colleagues in Montpellier suffered from the heavy taxation of products from the Orient. Jean-Louis Fargeon remembered his father's words. He would have to leave to escape decline.

The motto of the newspaper *Mercure de France*, taken from Virgil, *mobilitate viget* (only through action can one thrive), finally convinced him to leave Montpellier. The May–June 1770 issue included a description of the festivities and ceremonies held on the occasion of 'the arrival of Madame l'Archiduchesse Marie Antoinette in France and of her marriage to Monseigneur le Dauphin. Madame la Dauphine must have noticed, as she travelled through France, the pressing enthusiasm of the French to see her, admire her, love her,' reported the *Mercure*. The young perfumer from Montpellier also read the compliment of Sieur Bignon, provost of merchants, upon the future Queen's arrival in Paris: 'You shall delight France with your style.' Fargeon studied her portrait, amid the floods of praise, including a poem by Sicard de Roberti that seemed to allude to the perfumer's art:

> *The fragrance of your bouquets led me momentarily to believe*
> *That they were composed of a thousand new flowers,*
> *With haste I opened your basket,*
> *Only to find that they were immortal.*

Rumours from the Court eventually began to circulate in Montpellier. It was said that upon Marie Antoinette's arrival in France, the Comtesse de Noailles had been appointed lady in waiting to the Princess, who immediately nicknamed her

'Madame Etiquette'. This French version of a Spanish *duena* was a stickler for the strict observance of proper conventions and customs. One of her contemporaries asserted that she was living proof that 'a certain reserve and great social grace can compensate for the lack of a mind'.[14] 'Madame de Misery', the Princess's First Lady of the Bedchamber, was also keen on etiquette and was appalled to hear the young Austrian burst out laughing, like a bourgeoise of the Marais. Some found Marie Antoinette's wit to be mocking, sometimes cutting, and it was said that she took after her father, François, Duc de Lorraine, who was so adamantly French that he refused to learn the German language of his wife, the Empress of Austria, and who had earned a reputation as a rather shallow man with a pronounced taste for pleasure.

The future Queen of France was the very image of Fargeon's perfect client – young and beautiful. At fifteen she had been described by Madame Campan as 'bursting with freshness, more than beautiful in the eyes of all. The way she walked was a combination of the proper posture for princesses of her house and French gracefulness; her eyes were soft, her smile sweet.' It was said that her marriage to the Dauphin had boosted Paris's luxury trade beyond the wildest expectations of its merchants, and it was overheard in the Fargeon boutique that the question of make-up was discussed even at the Ministry of Finances. According to custom, the great ladies were heavily made up whenever there were presentations at Court, and as the number of presentations increased, one producer of rouge, in anticipation of the resultant sales, offered five million livres to obtain the exclusivity of his product.

Paris was without question the only place where the creative gifts of a young perfumer could be recognized and recompensed. The centre of taste and elegance was there, and a wonderful muse had just arrived. Fargeon told his mother of his plans, perhaps praising the Princess in much the same terms as those of the Marquise de Durfort: 'She has a charm that will turn our heads, to say nothing of her face, which I find lovely.'[15]

The excellent reputation of Montpellier's House of Fargeon had travelled as far as Paris, where a Fargeon cousin exploited it at a perfumery called Oriza, a boutique installed in the privileged and enclosed area of the courtyard of the Louvre. The cousin had established Oriza there because he had not been received into the community of perfume and glove makers; here he could do business without being subject to the visit of their masters or to their jurisdiction. The products of the House of Oriza nevertheless had a certain renown, and its preparations designed to improve the freshness of the complexion, made for the famous Ninon de Lenclos, were particularly popular. Through this Parisian branch of the family, Jean-Louis was informed that he could pursue and perfect his apprenticeship with the widow of Jean Daniel Vigier, née Marie Geneviève Boutron, in the rue du Roule in the parish of Saint-Germain l'Auxerrois.

He considered the fact that the boutique was located near the church that had celebrated the Dauphin's nuptial mass as a promising sign. His mother was also reassured upon learning that he would be close to the merchants from Provence who sold *eaux de fleurs d'oranger* and other strong or sweet essences to customers in the quarter known as the *cul de sac des Provençaux*, near the cloister of Saint-Germain l'Auxerrois. All this was excellent news. The late Jean Daniel Vigier had been an ordinary perfumer to the King and a member of the prestigious Parisian community of perfumers. His clientele had included the beautiful courtesan Madame Du Barry and other celebrities of the Court and of the city. His widow was the descendant of a prominent family of perfumers and was known as an excellent businesswoman. And so a contract was agreed upon between the two widows: Jean-Louis would pass the year of preparation for his *maîtrise* with the widow Vigier.

The conditions of the agreement, as laid out in the statutes of the Communauté des Gantiers Marchands Parfumeurs, were standard for an apprentice at the time. He would respect his master 'as if he were his father', he would keep the required secrets regarding all his activities, establish and maintain good relations with his companions and prove himself 'clean and modest'. It was agreed that the sum the Fargeons would pay would be part of an annuity of 40,000 livres, which would count towards the price of the business which the young perfumer would acquire upon completing his *maîtrise*.

❧ A Parisian perfumery ❧

In early 1773 Jean-Louis took the stagecoach to Paris, his only possessions being his twenty-five years, an agreeable bearing and an already impressive professional savoir-faire.

Paris deserved its nickname, 'the city of mud'. The Gobelins river, the hospitals and the workshops dumped all manner of filth into the polluted Seine and the stench from the cesspools was unbearable.

The rue du Roule, where the boutique was located, was 'adequately wide, bordered by houses occupied by all kinds of merchants, seemed one of the most crowded and teeming of Paris',[16] and the four-storeyed Vigier home at number 11 was identical to the others facing the street, with its dormers, its gables and its balconies. This regularity was the fruit of the housing plan of 1691 for the area which had previously been occupied by the Hôtel de Maisons. At first glance, the boutique was not so very different from Fargeon's father's in Montpellier, but everything here was more refined and delicate. The walls were covered with wood panelling painted pearl white, with porcelain-blue highlights. The mahogany shelves reached to the ceiling, which was decorated with cherubs frolicking in a *trompe l'oeil* sky. Small bottles, toilet articles, gloves, garters, and everything an aristocratic woman could need overspilled the shelves. A subtle scent of flowers erased the fetid smell of the air from the street.

The mistress of the shop explained to Fargeon at length all that he could expect. The business was doing very well, but demanded a good deal of prudence and discernment. She proudly cited the names of her most illustrious clients, Madame Du Barry and the Princesse de Guéménée, a close friend of Marie Antoinette, whose entourage was already nicknamed 'the perfumed Court'. She confirmed that certain courtiers were in the habit of forgetting to pay their bills, hence the necessity to present them with polite firmness. Tastes were diverse and occasionally eccentric. The Comtesse de Sainte-Hermine spent a fortune on perfumed garters, while the Abbé d'Osmond had a weakness for violet powder that would be his ruin. Wealthy Parisians would perfume the walls of their rooms to mask the unpleasant odour of onion that came from the varnish that coated them and most used a different perfume for different moments of the day. The Comte de Fersen, who would later be Marie Antoinette's lover, had exclaimed on arriving in Paris, 'What a debauchery of jewellery and of perfume! And the bizarre odour of the salons of this country!'[17] The use of perfumes was spreading like wildfire among the elite of the city. Bailly, the perfumer who had introduced moulded cake soap and perfumed soap as early as 1713, had made a fortune and lived like a lord.

At nightfall, after a frugal dinner, the young apprentice arranged his few belongings in the small room on the mezzanine that would be his, and the next day he began to work with enthusiasm. The mistress of the shop was intent on introducing him to her clients, and Fargeon was amazed that such grand bourgeoises would bother to come to the shop in person. They liked to meet there, the widow Vigier told him, because it was something of a neutral ground, and they could speak freely since they knew that nothing said here would ever be repeated. She advised the young man to be every bit as discreet as she was.

In the days that followed, he discovered that Parisian women were entirely different to their counterparts in Montpellier – confident, flirtatious and brazen. In Montpellier, women of the upper classes behaved like prudes, and the nobility barely concealed their contempt for commoners. In Paris, although he was young and still occupied a junior position, the clients treated him courteously but Fargeon was horrified by the way they spoke of their peers once the latters' backs were turned. Madame de Marsan, governess to the daughters of the King, thoroughly condemned Marie Antoinette's taste for parties and fancy dress. 'La Du Barry', the King's mistress, was also the target of some savage epigrams. Indeed, no one hesitated to verbally commit the crime of *lèse majesté* by trouncing the King himself. Fargeon's father was right to have said that France had been ruined by these Court prebendaries, and that one day they would have to consider reforming, if not abolishing, the monarchy. The perfumer had always added with a smile that the Republic, as Monsieur de Montesquieu observed, was founded on virtue, but that that, alas, was certainly not the case when it came to the prosperity of the perfume trade.

❧ A visit to Madame Du Barry ❧

After he had been working for some time at the rue du Roule, Madame Du Barry requested that Fargeon be presented to her, having heard Madame Vigier praise his talents. Fargeon's first visit to Versailles filled him with wonder, but he could not have failed to notice the stench that also pervaded this most famous of palaces.

> The park, the gardens, even the chateau turn the stomach with their dreadful odours. The hallways, the courtyards, the buildings and corridors are filled with urine and faecal matter. At the very foot of the ministers' wing, a pork butcher bleeds his pigs and roasts them every morning. The Avenue de Saint-Cloud is covered with stagnant water and dead cats.[18]

When Fargeon was announced to Madame Du Barry, the King was with his favourite mistress who, for the sake of a lover's convenience, lived in the Petits Appartements on the second floor, just above his bathroom. The only place Fargeon had ever seen Louis XV was on coins and etchings. The Bien Aimé 'was still, in his old age, the most attractive man of the kingdom; his countenance was one of a perfect blend of grace and majesty; he was of an admirably proportioned height; his expression was one of pride tempered by ineffable sweetness; there was nothing like the charm of his smile; his voice went directly to the heart'.[19] But by the time Fargeon walked into the boudoir, the King had slipped out by another door. The countess reclined upon a chaise, her head on her hand, exposing the most beautiful arm in the world.

Fargeon handed her a small vial of *eau de cypre composée*, whose jasmine, iris, angelica, rose and orange blossom were heightened by three nutmegs, blanched and crushed, and thirty drops of amber. Even those who detested the smell of amber found the scent pleasing.

'The Favourite' let a drop fall upon the back of her hand, then bent her lovely nose to smell it. She found it exquisite and Jean-Louis, encouraged, had her smell a more audacious composition. He had mixed citron, orange blossom and iris in an *eau de vie de Cognac* to which he had added mace and an ounce of daucus. After having recommended Balm of Mecca for the skin, he presented her with a collection of small pots of rouge in nuances of colour, of different tones for different occasions. He was especially proud of the nine shades he had obtained by increasing the amount of talcum powder by half an ounce each time, all the way to a tint of *déblanchi*, obtained by mixing a pound of talcum and a *gros* of carmine. He had added drops of olive oil to the gum so that the rouges would be uniformly smooth and the ingredients would not separate.

Finally he opened the little box containing black taffeta adhesive beauty spots in round, crescent, star and heart shapes, with a small metal puncher. Each spot served a purpose and had its own language. Placed next to the eye, a provocative mood was created; at the corner of the mouth it suggested the desire for a kiss; upon the lips it was mischievous and on the nose impudent. Haughtiness was suggested by placing one upon the forehead, flirtatiousness on the cheek, playfulness on the laughter lines, discretion on the lower lip, and perhaps deviousness when using one to hide a sapphire.[20]

Madame Du Barry wanted to accentuate the natural colour of her blond hair, and Fargeon promised to bring her a blend of saffron, turmeric, polypodium fern roots, St John's wort, gentian, citrin-coloured sandalwood and rhubarb. If she used the lotion regularly to wash her hair, it would be even blonder.

Their interview had gone on for over an hour, and the young perfumer was quite surprised to find before him a woman who in no way resembled the portrait her detractors had fashioned. The Duchesse de Choiseul, for example, had long ago refused the honour of being part of the King's inner circle rather than find herself in the company of Madame Du Barry. The Dauphine could not stand her and referred to her only as 'the creature'. Fargeon could not understand the severity of their judgement of a woman of whom the Marquis de Bouillé observed:

> There was nothing common or vulgar about her style; she may not have possessed a brilliant wit, but she certainly was not lacking in this domain to the extent that people enjoyed remarking. She liked to talk, and she had picked up the art of telling a good story. Kindness, that was her distinctive character trait. She was good, and she liked to please, she was not vindictive and she was the first to laugh at all the songs people made up about her. One only had to meet her once to perceive this dominant quality, one that no disappointment could have turned bitter. She had adopted the style and the manner of the ladies of the Court. Du Barry was an educated and well-read woman who had a noble air which made her even more irreproachably beautiful. She was a very interesting conversationalist, and, after the *toilette*, this was her principal occupation.[21]

❧ The confirmation of the Maître gantier parfumeur ❧

Jean-Louis passed his days studying to pass the *maîtrise*, poring over a thick book containing the statutes of the profession. No one could be confirmed as a *marchand maître gantier parfumeur* without having completed four years of apprenticeship followed by three years as a *compagnon*, in training. This did not apply to the sons of *maîtres*, but they were nonetheless required, as were the others, to produce a master work which, for them, was called an experiment.

After a good deal of reflection about what his experiment should be, Fargeon decided to perfect the *toilette à la mode de Montpellier*, a specially perfumed cloth, which also gave him the opportunity to pay homage to the work of his ancestors. Madame Vigier found this an excellent idea and spread the word among her clients.

Fargeon worked day and night on his *toilette*, so named for the cloth (*toile*) which was pulled tight across a table of marquetry or of precious wood and imbued with a delicate perfume. The key to perfecting the specially scented cloth lay not in the preparation of the material itself but in improving the composition of the precious blend in which it would be soaked by modifying the proportions of its ingredients, reducing some of them and increasing others. In this process, patience was essential.

In the hidden space of his laboratory, Fargeon wrote in his notebook of formulae:

> Begin with a new piece of fabric, not too tightly woven, cut to the appropriate size to make the specially perfumed cloth. Begin by flushing out the cloth, washing it several times in plain water. Stretch it out to dry, then soak it for twenty-four hours in toilet water, one part *eau d'ange* to one part *eau de roses*. Remove it and lightly wring out the liquid, then hang it up to dry in the air overnight. Dip it then in the following composition: half a pound of dried orange blossom, half a pound of campana root, half a pound of iris of Florence, four ounces of citrin-coloured sandalwood, two ounces of marc of *eau d'ange*, an ounce of rosewood, an ounce of souchet, half an

ounce of ladanum, half an ounce of cloves, half an ounce of sweet calamus and two *gros* of cinnamon. Reduce this mixture to a powder in a mortar, with tragacanth; add *eau d'ange* until it makes a paste. Rub the two sides of the cloth with it vigorously, leaving the bits of the paste which will stick to it, which will make it blend more uniformly. Allow it to half-dry, then rub the two sides again with a sponge soaked in *eau d'ange* or *eau de mille fleurs*, to make it fast. Let it dry for the last time, then fold it. The lining of this type of specially perfumed cloth is usually taffeta, and the right side of tabis or satin. It should be stored only between two pieces of silk.

For the second phase, take a pound of dried orange blossom, a pound of iris of Florence, half a pound of campana root, twelve ounces of marc of *eau d'ange*, two ounces of dried lemon peel, two ounces of souchet and an ounce of cloves, an ounce of dried orange peel, one of calamus, one of ladanum and an ounce of cinnamon water. Pound these into a thoroughly blended powder, placed in the mortar with a sufficient quantity of tragacanth, diluted with an equal portion of *eau de roses*. The result from mixing all these together is a perfect paste with which one can cover the two sides of the cloth, which I allow to dry and upon which I then reapply the following composition: I crush together in the mortar a *gros* of musk and a *demi-gros* of civet and, adding a spoonful of the above-mentioned paste, I mix it with toilet water to which I gradually add *eau de mille fleurs* or *eau d'ange*. Then I take a sponge and rub my cloth with this blend, making it as uniform as possible. This done, I finally let it dry for the last time. While it is still damp, I fold it in the proper fashion. The precious cloth, which gives its name to the *toilette*, is ready.[22]

Fargeon was so pleased with his recipe that he could not resist telling the widow Vigier, 'The trail of scent that lingers is marvellous. Lively and strong, it perfumes the air but is not oppressive. I think it is wonderful.' He even thought of applying the innovation to a woman's négligé, with the idea that it would be stored in a *portefeuille*, a scented pouch that would renew the delicate fragrance every morning – an idea of minor importance, but one that would show off his savoir-faire.

The morning of 1 March 1774 was the day Fargeon was to pass his *maîtrise*. At the head of the community, four masters and jury members enforced the rules. Each jury member was appointed for two years and, each year, the two senior jury members were replaced. They were particularly interested in his new invention for the négligé and praised his initiative. After he was approved, the young man was brought with great ceremony to the Crown Prosecutor's office at Châtelet, where he was received as a master and took his oath, in accordance with Article 8 of the rules of the corporation. By virtue of the decree of the Council of 1745, he was declared *maître gantier parfumeur poudrier* and his name was inscribed upon the register.

Upon his return to the boutique, Madame Vigier included in her warm congratulations an allusion to the fact that it was now time for him to marry. He was of the same opinion, for no one could imagine keeping the shop alone. The widow, seeing that he was amenable to her suggestion, told him she had in mind a young woman from the parish of Saint-Eustache, Victoire Ravoisié, whose father, Guillaume Louis, was gunsmith to the King. Her mother, Françoise Charlotte Gouël, came from an excellent family; her eldest brother, Jean-Arnault, was an architect and the youngest, Gabriel-Louis, was a prosecutor at Châtelet. Madame Vigier emphasized the fact that the young lady had received an excellent education, had already assisted her mother in keeping the books at her father's shop and, quite obviously, would make a very good tradeswoman.

Jean-Louis Fargeon accepted the widow's suggestion and encouraged negotiations. Victoire Ravoisié's mother, discreetly questioned, provided attractive references: the family counted among its members a consul of the City of Paris, a buildings clerk, a jeweller to the King, a former surgeon-major and other relatives in the service of the King. The family's entourage included parliamentary counsels, stipend controllers and cloth merchants. On her side, the widow Vigier did not neglect to present Jean-Louis Fargeon's family in the most favourable of lights and to guarantee his maturity and his industry.

Once the ground was prepared, Jean-Louis went to mass at Saint-Eustache in the hope of glimpsing Victoire Ravoisié, and during the service, he had all the time he needed to observe her. Pretty but not beautiful, she carried herself with grace, and her abundant, golden-brown hair was modestly gathered up under a mantilla.

As soon as he had expressed his willingness to marry, Fargeon was invited to call at the rue Coquillère, officially, as a suitor. He immediately told his mother, knowing that such a match could only please her, and he began courting Victoire according to the custom, in the presence of a woman of the house, an aunt or a cousin. Since these chaperones often had other things to do, he would have passed long moments in the salon alone with his fiancée. Victoire admired her suitor who, with his elegance and his manners, bore little resemblance to the young men she usually encountered. She was curious about her future life which, she told him, would entail an enormous change from the world of her father's arms shop. Ever since childhood, she had been surrounded by swords and muskets. She knew nothing about perfumery but wanted to learn everything.

Fargeon may have launched into lyrical praise of his craft, much as he would one day write at the beginning of his definitive book on the subject:

> Among the arts that have been born of luxury and wealth, none produces more voluptuous sensations than that of the perfumer. Incessantly searching for the aromas exhaled by flowers, the peels and barks or the wood of some scented plants, he captures their odours in alcohols or oils or essences. He creates new fragrances according to his tastes, sensations that are most pleasing every day, and he brings into play together fragrances of all seasons, of all climates, and of all countries. A perfumer who wishes to excel in his art must possess theoretical knowledge, including the theory of odours, how to extract the substances that contain them, how to conserve them and blend them with others that show an

affinity, the knowledge of what effect these blends will have upon the sense of smell, which sensations are the most voluptuous, which the sweetest, and of the methods that have been used up until now to compose cosmetics and perfumes.[23]

II

The Touches
from the Heart
1774–1782

You who so love flowers, I offer you this bouquet.
LOUIS XVI to MARIE ANTOINETTE

❧ Queen of France, of Navarre – and of fashion ❧

The Comtesse Du Barry had promised the young perfumer that she would speak favourably of him to the King, to establish his merit at Court, but Louis XV would never hear this praise. Less than a month after Jean-Louis Fargeon was named a *maître*, one evening in April 1774, the King came down with a fever upon his return from a day of hunting. The doctors diagnosed smallpox, an illness that in those days one either survived or succumbed to after nine days. Jean-Louis knew of its ravages since he had invented treatments for the disfiguring pockmarks of the disease.[24] On 9 May the King received the last rites. His pustules, once dried, had given him, according to Madame Campan, the aspect of 'a Moor, a Negro, burnished and swollen'. The odour they gave off was unbearable. He died the following day.

In the rue du Roule, there was much talk of events at Versailles. A young *maître* assured all that a chambermaid had told him of the last encounter of the dying man with his favourite, Madame Du Barry, where the King had ordered her to leave Versailles. In tears, Du Barry had kissed his hand before leaving for her home in Rueil. Fargeon was disappointed to have failed when he had been so close to realizing his dream but there was still hope in the form of the new

33

Queen, who had a passion for perfume and a seemingly limitless fortune to spend.

෨෧

Louis XVI was only twenty years old, Marie Antoinette nineteen, when they inherited the throne. 'My God, guide us and protect us, we reign too young!' the new monarch exclaimed. From the moment of her coronation, the Queen would be hailed as a great beauty, her style emulated and her every move discussed, but, already, malicious couplets were circulating in Paris:

> *Little queen of twenty years*
> *You who treat people so badly,*
> *You will pass through the barrier again!* [25]

'They're laying into the Queen tooth and nail,' Fargeon read in Baudeau's *Nouvelles éphémérides* on the day the young sovereigns came to power, 'and there is no limit to the flood of horrors that pour forth. It's the Jesuit cabal of Chancelier Maupeou and the bigoted old aunts who are spreading these rumours to ruin her.' [26] Ill informed, the Empress wrote to her daughter, 'I cannot express my special joy at what we hear, the entire universe is ecstatic. And with reason! A king of twenty, and a queen of nineteen! All of their actions are full of humanity, generosity, prudence and good judgment.' [27] The 'little queen' treated these calumnies as a joke. In December 1775 she wrote to her mother, 'We are experiencing an epidemic of satirical songs. For myself, I have not been spared; I have been widely supposed to have two tastes, for women, and for lovers.' She was said to be having lesbian affairs both with her friend Madame de Lamballe and, just for good measure, with her milliner, Mademoiselle Bertin. These rumours were, to the young Marie Antoinette, far too silly to upset her. Who would have dared to deny the amusement of a young, vivacious and pretty queen? Even the King never refused her wishes – Madame Campan asserted that he was a slave to all her desires.

The merchants following the Court seized the moment of the young couple's coronation. A jeweller had the idea of painting the portrait of the King and Queen on simple, shagreen-lined boxes. This little novelty was called a 'consolation for sorrow'. The milliner Rose Bertin invented a *pouf*, or headdress, that was perfect for the occasion. It was an extraordinary composition: on the left there was a grand cyprus dripping with black cares and worries, at the foot of which a black crêpe mourning ribbon represented a tangle of roots. On the right, a large sheaf of wheat lay upon a cornucopia from which spilled grapes, melons, figs and other perfectly realistic fruits, all of it interwoven with white feathers. The message of this work was that, while the pain of the loss of the King plunged its most profound roots into the hearts of his subjects, the new reign promised abundant riches. This allegorical *pouf* was rapidly replaced by the inoculation *pouf*. Louis XVI had been inoculated against smallpox on 18 June 1774, and the success of what was not yet known as a vaccination had inspired the milliner. Beneath a rising sun, she fashioned an olive tree laden with fruit about which twined a serpent supporting a bludgeon decked in flowers. In plain terms, the serpent Asclepius slaughtered the smallpox monster in the sunlight of the new King and in the peace symbolized by the olive tree.

❧

Two months after the death of Louis XV, the marriage of Jean-Louis Fargeon was celebrated at Saint-Eustache, the bride's parish, as was the custom. The matrimonial contract stipulated the goods to be held in common, both furnishings and property, as was traditional in Paris, and was notarized by Maître Paulmier on 26 July 1774.[28] The newlyweds were surrounded by their witnesses. Merchants, a Parliamentary lawyer, a former consul and a stipend controller stood up for the bride. Jean-Louis's witnesses were Louis-Sebastien Mercier, *maître ès art* at the university and future author of the well-known *Tableau de Paris*; Etienne Chaulair, painter to the

King; and Pierre Guiraud, doctor of medicine at the University of Montpellier.

The couple moved in above the boutique in the rue du Roule, in the apartment where the Vigiers had once lived. Victoire played her new role to perfection: she knew how to be amiable without being complacent and respectful without being fawning. The two talked about the future of their business, which was successful despite the stiff competition. This came partly from 'privileged' sectors – craftsmen and workers who, though they had not been confirmed as masters, were permitted to exercise the profession of perfumer in certain areas that were under close surveillance by police lieutenants.

Their professionally confirmed colleagues in the quarter of the Faubourg Saint-Honoré were even more worrying rivals. At the request of Colbert, the Minister of State under Louis XIV, Le Nôtre, the King's gardener, had cleared a perspective stretching from the forest of Boulogne to the crest of l'Etoile. Grand lords and financiers were building great mansions, with gardens that were an extension of those of the Champs Elysées, in this new part of the city. Perfumers were setting up shop in the area, to be near their clients. In 1775 a certain Jean-François Houbigant, who had enjoyed the patronage of the Duchesse de Charost, had opened a boutique, the Corbeille de Fleurs, at 19, rue du Faubourg Saint-Honoré. He had just created *l'eau d'Houbigant*, a scent both refreshing and sweet, composed exclusively of flowers. His way of marketing his product made it clear that he would be a formidable competitor: 'It is to the beauty of the face all that the morning dew is to flowers; it refreshes and stimulates the skin, while imbuing it with exquisite smoothness, lending it a most delicate velvety aspect and protecting the complexion from all ailments of the skin. Used in the bath, it renders the body its strength and stimulates vital energy.'[29] Houbigant also sold wig powder, *mille fleurs* extracts, gloves and fans, fragrant tablets to burn and, in homage to his patroness, a *pommade à la Duchesse*. It was said that he had sent two perfumes to the Queen, one named Marie Antoinette, the other Maria Teresa, but that the sovereign found the flattery too blatant and had not wished to accept them.

Fargeon had not forgotten his primary objective, which was to improve 'the sparkle of beauty with artistically prepared cosmetics and repair the wrongs of age or nature towards the sex whose sweetest pleasure is to please'.[30]

Shortly after their marriage Fargeon asked Victoire to submit to a grooming session in the manner of the Court. The perfumer thoroughly cleansed her skin with beauty lotion followed by an astringent, then took a brush and began with an expert hand to cover his wife's face with a very diluted white paste, explaining each gesture as he worked. The light had to be unequal and the white of the forehead should be brighter than everywhere else. Around the mouth, it had to be alabaster white. He explained that the skin must have the aspect of lacquer in order to cover the damage caused by the sun or, all too often, smallpox.

The shade of rouge would always be chosen according to the occasion and to the character of the client. The carmine for outdoors, perfect for a walk in the forest, would be dreadful in candlelight. The demi-rouge was only used for night-time. 'It is not pleasing to the eye to wear a shocking vermilion, for, after all, one doesn't make an instrument more attractive by demolishing it.'[31]

When he had finished, he outlined Victoire's eyes with a fine black line, and then he used a pomade to make her lips, her eyebrows and her eyelashes glossy, once he had gone over the latter with a tiny comb.

He explained that wealthy ladies had their hair styled and powdered every day by their chambermaids or by a coiffeur and wigmaker who inundated wigs and hair with powder, using a huge silk powder puff. The women held a large funnel, a *cornet à poudre*, before their faces to keep from suffocating in clouds of white. The most popular powders were those with an iris base, which were called *poudres de violette*.

While dismantling his work of art with the help of floods of rice water, Fargeon told Victoire that women concerned with their appearance should remove their make-up regularly, for it often contained corrosive mineral particles that could have deleterious effects if left on the skin too long.[32] It could be removed with pearl barley water, lentil or lily water, or lotion of milk or sweet or bitter almonds. Everything depended upon the skin type, and the same was true for the creams. Some required oil of sweet almonds, white balm or May butter, others cocoa, spermaceti or cold four-seed oil. He confided that he could not stand the practice, common at Court, of bringing out the aristocratic whiteness of the skin by accenting the line of a blood vein or two with blue. Nothing was more unnatural.

Victoire declared herself sufficiently instructed in the arts of aristocratic grooming. She was more interested in the commercial aspect of the business and encouraged her husband to open up branch shops in the provinces and abroad. The first of these were established in Nantes and Bordeaux, both of which had the advantage of being a jumping-off port for the Antilles. Fargeon arranged to be paid in exotic raw materials such as vanilla, from which he would extract a wonderful essential oil.

෧෧෧

England was all the rage at the time, with Voltaire in *Lettres Anglaises* praising the beauty of the country's gardens and the wisdom of its liberal and enlightened institutions. The Comte de Tilly found the women beautiful in general, with a few who surpassed all others elsewhere in their ugliness, and the men generally well dressed, even if an embroidered suit and a sword seemed to embarrass them rather than setting them off at their best.[33] The gentry's taste for luxury was legendary, and Fargeon realized that it would be possible to recruit a following of valuable clientele there. He decided to visit.

The English aristocracy were much more concerned with hygiene and cleanliness than their French counterparts. They washed their hands and faces daily and the entire body two or three times a week. Many actually owned a bathtub, for they considered bathing a complement to physical exercise.

England also had a long tradition where perfumes were concerned. The Court of Elizabeth I was fascinated with spices, balms and animal essences, all things imported from the Orient and from Arabia by Venetian ships. In 1730 a young Spaniard from Minorca, Juan Famenias Floris, made a name for himself with his famous Lavender, for which elegant London developed a passion. To this he added essences of lavender, bergamot, thyme or wild thyme, as well as rose and vanilla-scented creams – anything and everything that could please his refined clientele. Jean-Louis Fargeon called upon him and found some ideas in the young Spaniard's boutique of which he was determined to take advantage. He left England having made the contacts that would allow him one day to create a prosperous business there.

❧ The extravagances of Rose Bertin ❦

In Paris, the Queen, like Fortune, favoured the audacious. Rose Bertin's latest wild creation had had the effect of crowning her the greatest of all milliners. The woman from Picardie, born into a peasant family thirty years before, had come a long way since her engagement at twelve at Mademoiselle Pagelle's shop of fashions, the Trait Galant, where she was employed as a *saute ruisseau* – literally, a stream jumper – a delivery girl who brought dresses, in their twill covers, to clients. The Princesse de Conti, amused by the girl's prattle, had been responsible for her prodigious ascent. Her latest creation was 'a feather panache, that elegant young women wore at the back of the head'.[34] The name had been taken from an exposé that the Sieur Beaumarchais had just published, entitled 'Quès aco, Marin?', attacking the Sieur Marinthe. The pamphlet had met with such success among the always-ready-to-deride Parisian public that one day, walking in the

Palais Royal, the unhappy Marin was forced to quicken his steps, then flee before a crowd that incessantly jeered, 'Quès aco, Marin?' The meaning of the Provençal expression, 'what's this?', was explained to Marie Antoinette, and she liked to use it frequently among her close friends.

'La Bertin' took it into her head to build a new millinery construction composed of three feathers, planted behind the chignon. The hair was then piled high upon the forehead, with the help of huge hairpins, and curled at the ends. Several rows of huge curls were arranged at the back of the head. This hairstyle, which completed the *quès aco*, was called the *hérisson*, or hedgehog. The nature of fashion is ephemeral, but this was perhaps even truer when it came to hairstyles. The next to appear was the *pouf aux sentiments*, described by the Comtesse d'Adhémar as

> a coiffure which has taken the place of the *quès aco* and is far superior by the multitude of things that enter into its composition and by the genius required to vary them with art. It is called a *pouf* because of the variety of objects it can contain, and *aux sentiments* because all of them must be related to what one likes the best. Women unanimously adore the *pouf*, and everyone wants to have one.

The *pouf* could be a combination of the most diverse elements: fruit, flowers, vegetables, stuffed birds, dolls and all kinds of knick-knacks. It was also a way of stating one's tastes and feelings.

Marie Antoinette's favourite hairdresser, the famous Léonard, was an expert at placing the *poufs* of gauze, woven among the locks of the hair. One day he surpassed himself by putting eighteen metres of fabric into a single coiffure. The wealthy ladies of Paris fought to outdo one another with such extravagances. The Duchesse de Lauzun was seen at the Marquise du Deffant's with a *pouf* that displayed an entire landscape: a churning sea with ducks swimming near the shore, a hunter lying in wait, and at the top of the hairdo a mill, with the miller's wife flirting with a priest. Beneath the ear, one could glimpse the unsuspecting miller, pulling a stubborn donkey by the halter.

ॐ∽ॐ

Fargeon's perfumes would be decanted into small porcelain bottles belonging to his clients. Set in a motif of interlacing flowers and lines resembling the markings of shells, these ornamental *objets d'art* were decorated with miniatures with mythological, romantic or pastoral themes – such as Cupid and Bacchus, Vertumnus and Pomona, Harlequin and Gilles, the shepherd wooing his shepherdess – domestic animals or exotic birds, along with romantic mottoes in gold letters: 'I am faithful', or 'Love wanes, friendship endures', or 'Freedom makes me faithful'. A masked Cupid beat a drum like a recruiting sergeant above the slogan 'I am signing up hearts'. The perfumer enjoyed deciphering the puzzles depicted on some of the bottles: a golden glory translated as 'I wore my glory to love'; a woman tucking her skirts up high to search for a flea in her garter was underscored with 'I envy his lot'. There was also the one where a bawdy monk carried a sheaf of wheat on his back to the monastery, the lower part of a beautiful woman, quite naked, sticking out of it.

Madame de Pompadour had reintroduced the old tradition of engraving on fine stone, and most of the bottle cases and holders were also decorated with cameos. The toilet kits were covered in shagreen, the name given to shark skin. Since 1750 the discovery in England of lead crystal had made it possible to turn out perfume bottles with gold or silver fittings in large quantities. The nobility wore only the most refined perfumes; there were marquises in a cloud of amber, young dandies smelling of cyprus, magistrates wearing enough musk to pass for weasels. Moralists denounced this riot of scents, but those who coveted the perfumes, make-up, unguents and powder scarcely paid them any attention.

❧ 'Heavy on the rouge!' ❦

Where fashion was concerned, everyone imitated the Queen, even down to her gestures and the way she expressed herself. She was the equivalent of today's celebrities, observed and admired by society in every capital from Madrid to St Petersburg. Those deprived of the privilege of watching Marie Antoinette learned of her style in the articles of the *Journal des dames.*

The Empress Maria Teresa, however, was irritated by her daughter's status as fashion icon and became angry when she saw a portrait of the young sovereign. 'No, this is not the portrait of a queen of France,' she exclaimed, 'there has been an error. This is the portrait of an actress!'[35] As for the Emperor, he criticized his sister for having introduced too many new fashions and

> tormented her about the use of rouge, to which his eyes could not become accustomed. One day, when she applied more than usual, before attending a performance, he advised her to add more and, gesturing towards a lady in the room who, indeed, wore a great deal, 'A little more under the eyes,' said the Emperor to the Queen, 'heavy on the rouge, like Madame.' The Queen begged her brother to stop making jokes and, especially, to reserve them for her company alone.[36]

Marie Antoinette's only consistent passion was for flowers, whether roses, jonquils, lilacs, violets or lilies. Otherwise, her tastes and interests changed from one moment to the next. One day in the summer of 1775, she presented herself before the King in a dress that, he exclaimed, was 'the colour of fleas'. The colour (puce) immediately became all the rage in Paris and in the provinces, and the fabric dyers created a variety of shades: old and young flea, flea belly, back or leg. A newcomer to the Court heard this advice: 'Wear a puce suit, a puce jacket, and show yourself with confidence.'[37] On another day Marie Antoinette, all dressed in green, preferring to confine her interests to clothes rather than affairs of the realm, encountered the influential Comte de Maurepas, secretary of the Royal Household. 'Can't you see to what simplicity I have kept?' she said. 'Here I am, all in one colour, all the way to my slippers of plain green satin.' Maurepas replied with a deep bow, 'I am no longer surprised to see the universe at your feet'[38] – a clever play on the words 'plain green' (*vert uni*) and 'universe' (*univers*). We can only guess what stories lay behind the shades of 'shy salmon' and 'chamois'. Once the King found a certain fabric whose colour reminded him of the Queen's ash blond hair. One of her locks was immediately sent to Gobelins and another to Lyon, to imitate the shade. Silks, velvets, even ratine and draperies, suddenly sold only in this colour.

Accusations of frivolity, which would ultimately bring such harm to Marie Antoinette, began to shake the throne. She was said to be 'extravagant like a fashionable woman or a favourite mistress, but not like a sovereign'. In 1776 the King, without batting an eye, paid off out of his own privy purse 487,000 livres of debts that she had already contracted, and the word spread that the ladies of France were going to ruin themselves trying to imitate the Queen. The Comtesse d'Adhémar made a plea, in reality an accusation against her mistress, all the while believing she spoke in her defence:

> The warm affection she showed concerning everything to do with her grooming was a clever means of keeping all intriguers away from her person. To all outward appearances, her only occupation was to decide on the number, the colour and the dimension of the feathers that immediately became the basis for every coiffure at Court. The feathers that were suddenly in style because of the Queen caused an absolute furor. They decorated hats and bonnets with a kind of extravagance. The carriages were no longer high enough: either the seats had to be lowered, or one had to kneel in them, and with the covered ones, this was impossible.[39]

There were cartoons of and pamphlets against feathers, and the royal ladies were not the last to cast blame upon this whim.

Fargeon wanted to highlight Marie Antoinette's beauty in a less ostentatious, more natural way. He was anxious to gain the favour of the Queen but often wondered if she might find offensive the brief favour accorded him by Madame Du Barry, the woman she had referred to as 'the creature'. However, one of his clients, the Princesse de Guéménée, had just inherited the position of governess to the Children of France (the royal children) and Fargeon saw this as his chance to establish himself at Court.

The Princesse de Guéménée was also a member of the intimate entourage of the Queen and gave spectactular parties in Paris and at her estate at Montreuil. While the King would retire every evening at precisely eleven o'clock, the Queen, when she did not go to Madame de Lamballe's, went to spend the evening at Madame de Guéménée's, where she was sure to find the Comtesse de Polignac. Yolande de Polignac had fascinated her since their first meeting, perhaps because 'her walk had the mark of seductive abandon' and because 'her movements were of a casual grace that made her stand out in the midst of the most beautiful women'.[40] The Queen adored the way she let fly with a witty quip and would drop in to see her, having supper there whenever she felt like it or when she did not go to see Madame de Lamballe, who tried her best to outdo her rival. At the Princess's, there were parties of lansquenet (a card game), singing and harpsichord playing, jesting and, especially, a good deal of talk. There was also gambling for high stakes, and the house, as Joseph II was said to have remarked on his trip to France, sometimes 'looked like a real dive'. At one of these all-night parties, the Queen played faro until four in the morning, and the following night until three. Louis XVI did nothing about it. 'The King, who never leaves his apartments in the evening and does not care for gambling, never mentions it on these occasions, noted Mercy, since he carries kindness to the utmost in allowing everything that may amuse the Queen.'[41]

One day when he was delivering the Princesse de Guéménée's purchases, Fargeon admitted to her that he had been dreaming of winning the Queen as a client. The Princess told him to send one of his products to her and she promised to recommend it to Marie Antoinette. Looking for something unique, Fargeon decided upon gloves. Like every well-bred man, he knew the significance of the glove. The object that one pretends to forget when one wants to be called back carries one's brand, one's perfume, one's stamp. It hides the hand that offers itself or withdraws.

The Queen liked to wear light-coloured gloves with her outfits. She ordered no fewer than eighteen pairs a month, all white or pearl grey, from Sieur Prévost. Perfumed gloves were a Montpellier speciality, but Fargeon would not limit himself to adding perfume, like his competition. He knew the secrets of crafting gloves, how to choose and treat skins, the best way to dye them in every shade.[42] It would be easy for him to distinguish himself from the competition in this respect and to create the *gants de la reine* the Queen could wear for riding. She liked to ride, was happy to put on a hunting habit, and her horse wore the magnificent saddlery of the Hungarian Gardes Nobles (aristocratic guards). Her mother Maria Teresa wrote in vain that 'riding is bad for the complexion'. In reality, she was afraid that this exercise would prevent the Queen from providing the realm with an heir. Marie Antoinette knew this, and it irritated her. The real obstacle lay not in the perils of horseback riding but in the indifference of the King.

Fargeon chose a chamois-coloured kidskin he felt would match the costumes of the Queen's equerries. White gloves were in style, and the upper classes wore nothing else, but the Queen pioneered fashion and was thus entitled to do as she pleased. To perfume the gloves, he chose the simplest of flowers: violets, hyacinths, blood-red carnations and musk jonquils known as *jonquilles à la reine*. They had to be picked in dry weather, an hour after dawn or before dusk. It was important not to crush them and to 'leave no green on the violet and half cut the stems of the tuberoses'.[43] This would guarantee a pure and natural scent. The gloves were then placed *en fleurs*, that is, arranged in cases between two beds of fresh flowers for eight days, so that they would be perfectly permeated with their scent. The perfumer dipped them in a preparation that served to preserve the softness and freshness of the skin of the hands and to protect them from the harsh contact of the reins. He coated the kid gloves with a mixture of pure white wax, sweet almond oil and *eau de rose*, then spread them out on a bed of fresh roses with a strong nutmeg accent to their scent, so they could drink in the odour one last time. After this treatment, they would have the same restorative qualities as the so-called cosmetic gloves designed as a beauty treatment for the hands at night.

❧ The kindness of the Queen ❧

A few days after he had delivered the gloves, Fargeon received an order for several identical pairs as well as others in pastel shades from the Queen's *dame d'atours* (the lady charged with clothing and accessories). Madame de Guéménée, who brought him the good news, advised him to wait for the Queen to pass on her way to mass to thank her for her kindness. She assured him that she would tell the Queen he would be there.

The following Sunday he left for Versailles. The ceremony was always the same: the Queen's ladies gathered first in the salon outside her bedroom, crowding together. This was no mean feat, for they were numerous, and all of them wore *robes à panier*, dresses whose bouffant skirts fell over whalebone frames. Then the Princesse de Lamballe went into the Queen's chamber, where she was busy with her *toilette*. After a few minutes, an usher would announce in a loud voice, 'Le service!' At this point, the four chosen ladies of the palace and a few others who had come to pay court would enter the chamber. In the gaming room, where the Queen would pass on her way to mass, a few privileged individuals, who had already been received in private audience or who presented others the Queen had not met, were allowed entry.

The audience dragged on until 12.40. Then the door opened and the usher announced 'The King!' Louis XVI joined the Queen, and the cortège assembled to go to mass. The First Gentleman of the Bedchamber, the captain of the guard and several other officers of the guard walked before, with the captain of the guards closest to the King. Then came the King and the Queen, walking slowly enough to say a passing word to the many courtiers who lined the way all along the great hall.

As Fargeon watched her walk towards him, he was so intent on drinking in every detail of the lovely vision his future client presented that he forgot to even look at the King. Her walk and her comportment were dignified and graceful. She had a sparkling complexion, and the way she held her head was admirable. She greeted those she wanted to single out in passing and, before she arrived at where he stood, he heard her say a few friendly words to people who had been recommended to her. He watched her approach, look at him carefully and smile as though she had just recognized him. Then she walked on, but this was already a strong sign of her favour.

Madame de Guéménée congratulated Fargeon when he went to thank her and informed him that the Queen had asked for something to add to her bath.

The perfumer personally delivered the sachets containing his preparation to Versailles, explaining its ingredients: four ounces of blanched sweet almonds,[44] a pound of *énula campana*, a pound of pine nuts, four handfuls of linseed, an ounce of marsh mallow root and an ounce of lily bulb. He also explained how to use it in the bath, recommending heating water from the river, preferably water that had passed through the mill wheel, and, when it was warm enough, to throw in the sachet. The Queen should sit on the large sachet, and the two others, which also contained some bran, should be used to rub her body. He knew the name of his preparation, *bain de modestie*, would please the woman who proclaimed that she detested pomp and etiquette.

The ladies responsible for the bathing and drying of the Queen received him well, for word of his favour was spreading throughout the Court. The bathroom was on the first floor, behind the Queen's chamber, near the Salon de la Méridienne. The floor was tile-covered and slightly sloped so the water would drain off. Hot and cold running water came through pipes from the cistern room situated just below. Fargeon was struck by the simplicity of the place. There was none of the elaborate décor the Rousseau brothers had created for Louis XV's bathroom, which was now the King's coffer room.

The head bath attendant explained to Fargeon that the Empress had taught her daughter to bathe regularly because, in Austria, hygiene is very important. In the upper classes, the bath was followed by rubbing the body vigorously with a washcloth soaked in bran water, but if this Spartan treatment was appropriate to the education of a princess, it was not suitable for a queen. Refined to the point of having had mahogany *lieux à l'anglaise* (hence loos) with an ingenious little jet of water installed in her apartments, the Queen took perfumed baths. According to Madame Campan, one detractor – a certain Soulavie – took this as a pretext to write that she had 'received a venerable old ecclesiastic while in her bath in the nude'. She took her baths wearing a loose-fitting flannel chemise that buttoned at the collar and cuffs. When she stepped out of her bath, the head bath attendant held a towel high and then threw it over her shoulders. The other bath attendants wrapped and dried her, and then she put on a long, open shift, heavily trimmed in lace, and a bed jacket of white taffeta, with lace-trimmed bath slippers. The wardrobe attendant warmed the bed and, dressed for the night, the Queen would get into it. The bath attendants and the boys would then take away everything that had just been used for the bath, while the Queen took up a book or her needlework. On bath days, she even had lunch on a tray arranged on the bathtub.

Fargeon believed that bathing contributed to feminine beauty. Each individual had their own bathing preferences.

Some bathed every eight days, others every two weeks, others once a month, and many only once a year for eight or ten consecutive days, at the best time of year to do so. One could bathe at home or at public baths, where all the conveniences were available, and where body hair could be removed in perfectly safe conditions. There were those who preferred what were termed domestic baths, because one could take them without leaving the house. There were three types of bath. The first involved the total immersion of the body, up to the neck. In the second, the demi-bath, the bather was seated in water that did not rise much beyond the navel. The third was a foot bath, where the water level stopped at the calf.[45]

Fargeon soon learned how the Queen's *toilette* proceeded. After an initial private phase, the *toilette de représentation* (the *toilette* at which people might be presented to the Queen) took place at noon. The piece of furniture known as the dressing table (in French *toilette*, the origin of the word) was placed in the middle of the bedroom and the Queen used it in the same place for undressing in the evening. Her peignoir was presented by the First Lady of the Bedchamber, if she was alone at the beginning of the *toilette*, and the other ladies in waiting presented the other objects as they arrived. At noon, the ladies who had served for the past twenty-four hours were replaced by two women in formal dress. Important visitors were admitted during the *toilette*, and folding stools were placed in a circle for the superintendant, the ladies of honour and the *dames d'atour*, and the governess of the Children of France, when she was present.

The ladies of the palace began their service when mass began; they waited in the grand chamber and entered only when the *toilette* was finished. The princesses of royal blood, the captains of the guard, all of those appointed to important positions and consequently allowed entry, paid court during the hour of the *toilette*. The Queen nodded to them or bowed slightly, leaning on the dressing table, to indicate her permission for them to rise; this last response was reserved only for princes of royal blood.

The King's brothers usually came to pay court to Marie Antoinette while her hair was being done. During the first years of the reign, dressing her took place in the chamber and followed the rules of etiquette. The lady in waiting dressed her in her chemise and poured water for her to wash her hands; the *dame d'atours* put on the petticoat of the dress or of the ceremonial garb, then the fichu, and tied or fastened the collar. But the coiffures and headdresses were so high that the chemise had to be stepped into. When the Queen ultimately requested the presence of Mademoiselle Bertin at her dressing, and the ladies refused to share this honour with her, the *toilette* no longer took place in the Queen's chamber, and the Queen, after greeting the assembly, retired to her private rooms to dress.

The dressing of the Queen was a masterpiece of etiquette, with rules for everything. The lady in waiting and the *dame d'atours*, if they were there together, were assisted by the First Lady of the Bedchamber and two ordinary women, responsible for the main service, but there were distinctions between them. The *dame d'atours* put on the petticoat and presented the dress. The lady in waiting poured the water for the Queen to wash her hands and put on her chemise. But when a princess of the royal family attended the dressing, she replaced the lady in waiting to accomplish the latter task. However, the lady in waiting did not cede her place directly to the royal princess; in this case, she gave the chemise to the First Lady, who then presented it to the princess of royal blood. All of the Queen's ladies in waiting scrupulously observed these customs and jealously guarded their rights of duty. One day in winter, the Queen was already undressed and about to put on her chemise. Madame Campan unfolded it and held it out. The lady in waiting entered, hurriedly removed her gloves, and took the chemise. There was a knock at the door, and Madame la Duchesse d'Orléans walked in. Once she had taken off her gloves, she went to take the chemise, but the lady in waiting should have given it instead to Madame Campan, who in turn would give it to the Princess. Another knock at the door heralded the Comtesse de Provence. The Duchesse d'Orléans gave her the chemise. The Queen held her arms crossed against her breast and appeared to be cold. Madame saw her pained expression, kept her gloves on and threw down her handkerchief to pass the chemise, but in doing so messed the Queen's hair. The Queen began to laugh to hide her impatience, but only after having said through clenched teeth, several times, 'It's odious! What a bother!'[46]

The *dame d'atours* had under her command a first chambermaid to iron and fold the articles for the *toilette*, two wardrobe valets and a wardrobe boy. The wardrobe boy delivered to the Queen's apartments green taffeta-covered baskets containing the things she would wear that day; he then brought the First Lady of the Bedchamber a book containing swatches from the dresses, ceremonial garb and négligés. A small bit of the trimming indicated the type of gown. The First Lady presented this book when the Queen awoke, with a pin cushion. The Queen would place pins in the swatches of all the things she wanted to wear that day: one for the ceremonial garb, another for the afternoon négligé, another for the evening gown she had chosen for cards or games or supper in the private apartments. The book was returned to the wardrobe, and soon the Queen's choices arrived, wrapped in taffeta. The wardrobe lady brought a covered basket with a choice of two or three chemises, handkerchiefs and a scrub cloth. The morning basket was called the 'ready for day', the evening one – containing the camisole, the night cap and stockings for the morning – was called the 'ready for night'. Once the *toilette* was finished, the valets and wardrobe boys would enter to return the unused articles to the wardrobe, where they were refolded, hung, checked over and cleaned with such amazing care and order that the dresses, even those rejected, looked brand new. The wardrobe consisted of three large rooms lined with wardrobe cupboards, some with rungs, others with rails. In each room, there were large tables that served to spread out the dresses and costumes and to refold them. Upon her arrival at the Court of France, the Queen had inherited the great vermilion dressing table that had belonged to the Dauphine Maria Josepha of Saxony, preserved with the property of the Crown by order of Louis XV. This dressing table was refurbished for Marie Antoinette by the prominent Parisian goldsmiths Jacques and Jacques-Nicolas Roëttier.

For winter, the Queen normally had twelve ceremonial outfits, a dozen little dresses, described as fancy, and twelve elaborate dresses with skirts supported by whalebone frames or paniers, suitable for playing cards or games or for supper in the private apartments. The summer outfits were also worn in autumn, and all of them were removed at the end of each season, except for those Marie Antoinette was particularly fond of, which remained in the wardrobe. These totals do not include the dresses of muslin, percale or similar fabrics. They had only recently come into fashion and were not counted in the number of gowns for each season, since they could be worn for several years.

๛

As soon as he had returned to his boutique, Jean-Louis Fargeon began to work on another original composition that blended incense, myrtle and spikenard in oils of blueberry, quince or water lily. He formed it into tiny balls which, he asserted, were 'good for cleansing and whitening the skin, leaving it with a pleasant scent'.[47]

For months he had supplied only gloves and sachets to Marie Antoinette, but, since perfumery naturally went with the grooming of hair, Victoire suggested he approach the celebrated Léonard, coiffeur to the Queen, and emphasize the fact that in Montpellier he had studied the powders and pomades designed for hair care, and thus could be of use to him. Léonard's art involved placing a bouffant shape made of horsehair and gauze on the head of the client, then brushing the hair up to cover it completely, using a pomade as well. Then he powdered the creation with perfumed starch and added spangles.

Fargeon had no difficulty arranging an introduction to the coiffeur through a client, on the pretext of admiring his work. In Léonard he found the personification of one of the little, beribboned marquises Molière used to make fun of. 'I work with the comb and the mind,' he liked to say repeatedly, pompously proclaiming himself 'Academician of coiffures and fashion'.[48] The perfumer explained that he presented no competition whatsoever but could prove a useful ally. Far from infringing upon the territory of the coiffeurs, he could work to their advantage by providing products of finer quality than they were used to working with. Léonard allowed himself to be convinced by Fargeon's argument.

In fact, their collaboration was more advantageous to the coiffeur than to the perfumer. Léonard was extraordinarily mean and never had the funds to pay his bills. 'Later, later!' he would fuss, the moment the matter was raised. He appreciated Fargeon's pomades and powders and praised them to everyone, but he always found a way not to pay for them. As was the case with Mademoiselle Bertin, the Queen's favour had gone straight to his head. Most of the time, to avoid the issue of his account, he sent round the handsome Julien, his first assistant, 'a character who was rather impressive and rather ridiculous, and beginning to become spoiled himself'.[49]

❧ Connections with Mademoiselle Bertin ❦

The collaboration with Léonard eventually proved fruitless, so Fargeon decided to seek the approval, if not the protection, of Mademoiselle Bertin. This was no easy matter, for the milliner, according to the Comtesse d'Adhémar, 'treated princesses as her equals'. The few times he had seen her in passing, she had never seemed to notice him. And so he was amazed when, one fine morning, she walked into his boutique with a decided air, followed by a lackey carrying a large, polished wooden box. She announced that he had been recommended to her by Madame de Guéménée and opened the box, which contained several varieties of extremely beautiful flowers. She explained that the flowers, made in an Italian convent, owed nothing to nature. They were made of fine batiste, taffeta and plastered gauze. All that was missing was their perfume, which she wanted Fargeon to provide. The milliner told him about the Queen and spoke at length of her kindness and her enthusiastic taste for all that was new. She suggested they present her daily with a new and original creation. Through his frequent visits to add perfume to Mademoiselle Bertin's artificial flowers, Fargeon became familiar with her superb shop, Au Grand Mogol, where she employed about thirty workers. Anyone who was anyone was seen in her salons where, on the pretext of shopping, one could rub elbows with society. She had developed the custom of using dolls as fashion mannequins, ones dressed in the latest Paris styles, which crossed France's frontiers every month to show the European courts the masterpieces of French elegance. Through this ingenious practice, 'La Bertin' had acquired a clientele that included nearly all of Europe's royalty.

Fargeon got to know her better. She was whimsical and disorganized, but a loyal friend. She treated him as the artist she considered herself also to be, capable of showing his work off to its best advantage. She was overflowing with ideas, often excellent and sometimes eccentric, that she incessantly sketched, but she was not particularly interested in managing her business and had never known the value of money. She could also be haughty and difficult. Her immense popularity had given her the impression that she could do anything she liked, and she even looked down on people of great rank. The Queen repeatedly quoted the line of King Prusias to her: 'Ah! Do not put me on bad terms with our nobility.'[50] The Baronne d'Oberkirch had summed her up with a cruel turn of phrase: 'This young lady's jargon is highly amusing, being a singular blend of haughtiness and vulgarity, which borders on impertinence when she is not kept in line, and which becomes downright insolent if one does not firmly put her in her place.' Everyone remembered her quarrel with Mademoiselle Quinault, which the Queen had settled. The actress, who had succeeded in marrying the Duc de Nevers, was one of the Court's darlings. One day she decided she would like a *pouf* on a sentimental theme and sent for the milliner, who refused to call on her. When the Duchesse de Nevers's chambermaid came to register her complaint, the milliner replied, 'Even if one is simply a creator of fashion, one does not bother to call on a former actress of the Opera when one has the honour of being employed by the Queen.'[51] The noblewomen had demanded her insolence be punished, and the Queen ordered her milliner to go and apologize. She had done so, and then she had taken to her bed for six weeks.

On another occasion, related by Madame Campan in her memoirs, the King and Queen were returning from their Easter greeting to their subjects when 'La Bertin' noticed Mademoiselle Picot, one of her former shop girls who had left to start her own rival boutique, in the crowd waiting to watch the royal couple pass. Enraged, she spat on her collar and said, 'I warned you, and I keep my word.' When a complaint was made against her, she attributed her 'involuntary gesture' to her 'disgust and revulsion'. 'I am not familiar with the lies of Mademoiselle Picot's clique and her friends,' she added, 'but I am morally certain that none of them stated nor could have stated that he saw me spit in Mademoiselle Picot's face. Me, commit such a base indecency!'

When Fargeon told his wife about the milliner's escapades, Victoire raised her arms to the heavens. She was frugal by nature and, even though the business was going well, she felt that a merchant should never live extravagantly or inspire envy. Nevertheless Fargeon's boutique had won favour at Court. He was purveyor to most members of the royal family, and composed preparations made for each of them individually.

The King's aunts were among his clients. They lived on the ground floor of the chateau at Versailles, and the largest room of their apartment looked out both on the terrace of the Parterre d'Eau and on the Parterre du Nord. He would often find them peeking through the windows to spy on the goings on at the chateau or plunged in conversation with one nobly born gossip or another who had brought fresh rumours from the Court. Occasionally when visiting the aunts, Fargeon had to wait for the departure of the King, who had come to listen to their advice, and patiently sit through their diatribes against the latest fashions, hairstyles and extravagances of their niece the Queen. They ordered articles for the *toilette*, swan's down powder puffs or toothpicks, *eau de Cologne* and, in memory of Louis XV, *eau de fleur d'orange du Roy* and *eau de lavande*. But the aunts were stingy and their bills never amounted to much.

Crossing the filthy corridors and knocking at ugly little doors, the perfumer would also call upon the King's brother, the Comte de Provence, a good and faithful client. He had created the *poudre de Monsieur*, a more luxurious version of the *poudre à la Fargeon*, for him. The Comte and his wife were fond of the scent of orange blossom and of tuberose, and he was a great consumer of *eau spiritueuse de lavande*. In contrast to so many nobles, the King's brother paid his debts, and Fargeon was never obliged to play the scene of Monsieur Dimanche with him. The bills delivered to his concierge were paid promptly.[52]

෯෴෯

On his delivery trips to Versailles, Fargeon realized that once one got far enough from the areas that reeked of the stench of latrines, the chateau had its own specific and not unpleasant odour – a slightly fermented perfume with a hint of pepper and musk, one that did not exist anywhere else. Since space was limited, many nobles had to content themselves with inconvenient and poorly lit apartments under the eaves, but simply being at Versailles overrode any discomfort. After a while, Fargeon no longer got lost in the stairs and hallways, where the air was as glacial as a Siberian steppe in the winter. The Comte and the Comtesse d'Artois, as well as Madame Elisabeth and her lady in waiting, Diane de Polignac, lived on the first floor of the south wing of the chateau, looking out on the Orangerie. 'Although these apartments were vast, in reality they were just several closets whose light came from the hall and were thus very dark.'[53] The King's young sister, to whom Fargeon had been recommended by Madame de Marsan, was charming. Her orders were always for *eau de lavande, eau de Cologne* and *esprit de fleur d'orange* and he invented a special powder for the Comte d'Artois, which naturally could only be called *poudre à la d'Artois*. The Polignacs' apartment faced that of the Duc d'Orléans, just across the small Princes' Courtyard. Madame de Polignac was one of the rare ladies of the Court who did not use perfume. Fargeon found this deplorable, but he avoided her for another reason, since he knew she loved to target people's reputations with her poisonous arrows. The Princesse de Lamballe, Superintendent of the Queen's Household, was very well housed, as was Madame de Guéménée, her neighbour at the end of the south wing. After the long-awaited birth of Madame Royale in 1778, the latter became governess to the Children of France.

The deliveries to Versailles from the House of Fargeon were extremely varied; valets and assistants bent double under packages of articles for grooming and stylishness, lemon pomade, royal cream in jars or in sticks, double orange blossom pomade, lengths of English taffeta, toilet waters, tongue scratchers to preserve pleasant breath, toothbrushes, carnation powder, cucumber pomade, combs both fine and large toothed, sponges, pots of fine porcelain, embroidered and perfumed sachets, garters, peignoir ribbons, hairpins, swan's down powder puffs, pots of rouge, sponges for the beard, cosmetic or glazed gloves, assortments of beauty spots, *eau de mélisse, eau de vulnéraire*, boxes made of coral, and other trinkets.

Victoire made sure that nothing was missing and kept rigorous accounts. Her husband had cleverly classed their clients, whether noble or commoners, according to their punctuality in paying their bills. Among the good debtors were, of course, the Queen and her immediate entourage, the King's brothers, Madame Elisabeth and the jeweller Boehmer. The 'dubious debtors with whom one should not deal'[54] included few nobles, since the King disapproved of not paying one's debts. There were also bad debtors, like the Queen's reader, Mademoiselle Laborde, whose tastes exceeded her means, but whom it was important to please. This was also the case with the Duc d'Orléans and the hairstylist Léonard, to name but a few.

❧ The Queen's favourite perfumes ❧

The Queen's orders represented a considerable amount of trade – over 200,000 livres in the year 1778 alone – and all of the purveyors had to deal with the *dame d'atours*. Sometimes the Queen's Household had to ask for funds from the department of the King's Household in order to meet her creditors' demands. Fargeon was perfectly familiar with his client's tastes. Although seduced by luxury, Marie Antoinette also appreciated simple toilet waters, like the *eau de fleur d'oranger*, also called *eau du Roi*, that the late Vigier had named in honour of Louis XV. These scents were created by the distillation of a single sweet-smelling raw material of vegetal or animal origin, and were known to have a soothing quality. The Queen had remarked on the benefits of essence of lavender, very much in vogue for the past twenty years, and of essence of lemon. She had a few drops added to her bath and placed in earthenware dishes, to purify the air in her apartments. She chose vinegars seasoned with orange blossom or with lavender. Her servants always had little boxes called *vinaigrettes* at hand, to use in case their mistress had an emotional shock or a malaise. She preferred these to smelling salts made from crystallized tartaric acid imbued with distilled and rectified spirits of Venus.

For Marie Antoinette, Fargeon especially created rose, violet, jonquil or tuberose scents obtained by distillation in spirits of wine after prolonged infusion. He intensified them with musk, amber or opopanax. Since she had developed a penchant for concentrated perfumes, he created *esprits ardents* (passionate or glowing spirits), which she laughingly rebaptized *esprits perçants* (piercing spirits), the result of several successive distillations. They were very expensive, due to the increased quantity of raw materials required as well as the hours of labour necessary to produce them. The *dame d'atours* showed little concern about their cost and ordered them often, to perfume the air, as well as tablets to burn and *mille fleurs* pot-pourri.

The Queen kept her favourite perfumes in a lovely grooming cabinet. When she travelled, they were kept in a sumptuous *nécessaire* (toilet kit) outfitted with small bottles of faceted, coloured glass with silver stoppers. She loved the perfumed sachets then in fashion. Fargeon made them by covering a piece of Florentine taffeta with another piece of satin or of silk, according to the taste of the customer, and filling them with pot-pourri, or powders or cotton scented with aromatic plants. Marie Antoinette liked to present them to her friends as gifts, always taking care to match the scent to the personality of the recipient.

She took great care of her skin, cleansing it with *eau cosmétique de pigeon* and using *eau des charmes*, made with the moisture drops exuded by grapevines in May, as an astringent. The *eau d'ange* purified and whitened Marie Antoinette's complexion, which was much admired and had no need of the *eau de Ninon de Lenclos* which was supposed to conserve youth. She used *Pâte Royale* hand cream to keep her hands soft and to prevent chapping. She loved pomades scented with rose, vanilla, frangipane, tuberose, carnation, jasmine and *mille fleurs*. For her baths she used soap scented with herbs, amber, bergamot or pot-pourri, and she ordered powders and opiates to keep her teeth bright. The master perfumer invented a powder and a cream *à la reine* exclusively for her. She bought her rouge from Mademoiselle Martin, but Fargeon sent her a sample of a rouge pomade that was excellent for the lips. He never knew whether or not she used it.

In 1778 both the Queen and her perfumer were identically blessed. The happiest of events took place, both in the rue du Roule and at Versailles. Since her marriage, wicked tongues had spread the word that Marie Antoinette would never be a mother, and she suffered greatly from this. Mademoiselle Bertin suggested she say a novena to the Virgin of Monflières, in Picardy. It seemed to have worked, for the Queen discovered she was pregnant.

Fargeon's joy at the news that he was to be a father perhaps equalled that of the King. His first son, heir to the boutique and all his secrets, was named Antoine-Louis. Fargeon had taken advantage of the simultaneous pregnancy of his wife and Marie Antoinette to develop various preparations useful for pregnant women that he could propose to the Queen. The summer of 1778 was scorching. Marie Antoinette suffered from the heat and could not get to sleep without a long walk in the open air of the gardens where the musicians of the chapel softly played. To soothe her, Fargeon prescribed not only the *eau de la Reine de Hongrie*, but *eau de mélisse*, a blend of lemon, cinnamon, angelica, cloves and coriander, as well. He recommended exchanging the *esprits perçants* for *eau d'ange*, made according to his formula of iris, rosewood, citrin-coloured sandalwood, benzoin flower, calamus aromaticus and storax. He excluded musk from his preparations and added only a few drops of quintessence of amber, to bring out the other scents. He prepared sachets of this composition and told the Queen's staff to use them on a burner to rid the air of bad odours, aware of how much more sensitive the sense of smell became during pregnancy. And finally, he created an *eau de fraîcheur* and an *eau rafraîchissante* to protect the skin from the ill effects of the hot weather.

As soon as Marie-Thérèse de France was born, on 18 December 1778, the Queen asked Rose Bertin to make a brocade robe costing 500 livres to give to the Virgin of Monflières as an action of grace. The provosts of the merchants and the municipal officials of Paris delivered the city's traditional gifts to the King and Queen, as was the custom on the occasion of 'the opening of the Queen's belly', with great ceremony. Madame de Guéménée became the governess of Madame Royale and appointed Fargeon 'Purveyor to the Children of France'. On this occasion his gift was a large basket of scented taffeta, a green velvet mat for the dressing table, lined with taffeta of the same shade and trimmed in gold, as well as candlesticks for the *toilette*.

Marie Antoinette was determined that her children would have a less conventional and rigid education than had been the custom in the past. She explained to her mother:

> The way children are raised now, they are much less fussed over. They are not wrapped up the moment they can go outside, and, as they gradually become accustomed to it, they end up spending most of the time there. I think it is the best and the healthiest way to raise them. My child will stay downstairs, with a little barrier that will separate her from the rest of the terrace, where she can also learn to walk sooner than she would on the parquet floors.[55]

Fargeon emphasized to Madame de Guéménée the importance of teaching young children sound habits of cleanliness, and the Queen was favourably impressed with this advice when she heard of it.

A short while after the birth of the Princess, Léonard sent the handsome Julien to Fargeon to ask for his help. The Queen had summoned her coiffeur barely a week after she had risen from childbed, for she had found that she was losing her hair. Léonard was asked to come every morning to treat the royal head of hair. He used the perfumer's *pommade à la Fargeon*, but he wanted to know if there existed products that would prevent the loss of hair. Fargeon loaded his emissary down with ancient oils of violet, jonquil and jasmine for massaging the scalp, and added his 'powder to preserve and thicken the hair', explaining that it fortified the roots and had the added advantage of 'brightening the imagination and strengthening the memory'.

❧ A rapidly repaired state of ruin ❧

Absorbed by his work, Fargeon did not pay much attention
to his wife's concern that their wealthy clients paid their bills
with increasingly irregularity. Disorder and insouciance were
the dominant characteristics at Court, and although it was
not lacking in rich clients, the House of Fargeon was heading
for bankruptcy because it could not collect on its outstanding
bills. The Queen's Household owed the perfumer a substan-
tial amount. There were no longer funds to pay salaries and
raw materials, and the boutique was 304,000 livres in debt.
Bankruptcy was registered on 12 January 1779.[56] The House
of Fargeon had such an excellent reputation that the idea that
it should disappear was unthinkable. Fargeon remained cool-
headed. He had to pay off his creditors, including his father-
in-law, his brother-in-law and several suppliers (most of them
from Grasse, like the Tombarellis or the Escoffiers), and had
to collect on the outstanding bills. Most of the negligent debtors paid up, for they had no desire to deprive themselves of
the luxuries of the House of Fargeon. Eventually, the Queen's
Household and her entourage, the Comte d'Artois and the
Comte de Provence, the aunts, Madame Elisabeth and the Children of France all finally cleared the slate of long outstanding
debts to Fargeon. This misadventure proved instructive, for
Fargeon learned to diversify his clientele and his activities. He
began to sell his products throughout France and, thanks to
his shops in Bordeaux and Nantes, developed his trade with
England and the 'French islands of America' as well as the
young United States of America.

Eighteen months after Fargeon's near-disaster, in July 1780,
an agitated Léonard paid him a visit. Swearing the perfumer
to secrecy, he explained that, despite the massages, the situation with Marie Antoinette's hair loss had become alarming.
Fargeon recommended a new fortifying powder perfumed
with iris and a pomade containing essential oils of jasmine,

tuberose, citron and jonquil. The latter was the most difficult to work with, which increased the price of the product, but it was one of the Queen's favourites and had a lovely scent.

Either by coincidence, or owing to the effect of the powder and the pomade, the Queen's hair soon ceased to fall out. Léonard, reassured, told Fargeon of his plan to have Marie Antoinette adopt a *coiffure à l'enfant* he had created. Madame Vigée-Lebrun, the Queen's portraitist, insisted that it was she who had been the first to suggest that the sovereign appear with her hair framing her face. Horrified at first at the thought of her hair being cut so short, the Queen finally acquiesced. The *coiffure à l'enfant* immediately became the latest fashion.

Never one to be far from the epicentre of a revolution, Rose Bertin sought to attract attention, all the more so because she wished to present a relative for the post of governess of Madame Royale's wet nurses. She managed to receive a rare honour. In the euphoria of fatherhood, Louis XVI decided to endow a hundred young ladies with dowries and to attend their weddings at Notre Dame. The event is related by Madame Campan in her memoirs. The royal cortège of twenty-eight carriages left Versailles and made its way to the church. Just across from the Grand Mogol, Marie Antoinette looked up and saw Rose at her balcony, surrounded by her employees. 'Look, there is Mademoiselle Bertin!' she cried, and gave the milliner a little wave. Mademoiselle Bertin was in such favour that Madame Du Barry, anxious to come out of her retirement at Pont-aux-Dames, thought for an instant of asking for her intercession. In 1783 the celebrated milliner sold a bouquet of roses, globeflowers and carnations for thirty-six livres, a branch of white lilac for twenty-four. Her prices skyrocketed, and she charged an unbelievable 6,000 livres for a New Year's Day costume.

❧ The 'perfume of the Trianon' ❧

In the final, peaceful years before the Revolution, Marie Antoinette spent more time at the Petit Trianon, the former property of a royal mistress that the King had given her as a present in 1774. As Saint Simon described it, it had been a 'porcelain house for taking tea'. The Queen had accepted this gift with the sole intent of going there to 'have some repose from the fatigue of etiquette' and to live in this pastoral retreat 'not as a queen, but as an individual, away from the demands of things ceremonial'.[57] The architect Richard Mique and the artist Hubert Robert had seen to the reviewing and correcting of any foibles of nature. The King himself never went to the Trianon unless he was invited; he dined there, but never slept in the bedroom reserved for him. All the servants there belonged to the Queen. She was roundly condemned for this caprice and was accused, among other things, of having decorated an entire room with precious stones – in reality, a theatre made of tin, with stones made of glass. Her critics emphasized the extravagance of her royal whims: the Anglo-Chinese garden alone cost 300,000 livres merely in its preparatory stage. The concierge, Bonnefoy du Plan, lovingly kept a flower-bed of violets, the Queen's favourite flower, along with roses. In the spring, planting tubs, whose ornamental motifs Marie Antoinette had redrawn, were brought from the Orangerie and filled with rare species, imported at shocking prices: polygonums, Carolina catalpa, maple, larch, Judas tree, cedar, laburnum, oak from abroad, even a Virginia tulip tree, said to have come from America, having crossed the ocean on a three-masted schooner.

During the summer of 1780 Marie Antoinette launched a new fashion for dresses of white lawn, tied at the waist with a simple ribbon sash, modest, broad-brimmed straw hats and loose hair. Sticklers for tradition, like the Comtesse d'Adhémar, were offended by these 'children's dresses' or 'fruit-picking dresses', judged barely decent. Word spread that the Queen wanted to ruin the silk trade of Lyon and enrich the lawn makers of Brussels. Rose Bertin's provincial roots inspired her to create a *bonnet à la picarde*, which vied for popularity with the 'milkmaid's bonnet' and replaced the pompous 'insurgents' coiffure' invented by Léonard to honour the new United States of America. The royal shepherdess favoured soft, pale shades such as off-white, peach or sky blue. They were the colours that inspired the young Queen, who was happy to be a mother and in love with all things natural.

The royal family and that of the master perfumer grew at the same rhythm. Auguste-Frédéric Fargeon was born on 18 April 1781, and on 22 October of that year the Queen finally gave the kingdom a dauphin. Louis XVI was wild with joy, and representatives of the trade guilds of the capital – pastry chefs, masons, locksmiths, cobblers, even grave diggers – came to Versailles to congratulate him. Fifty market women from Les Halles, all of them dressed in black and most of them wearing diamonds, were presented to the Queen. Fargeon was part of the delegation of perfumers. He observed on this occasion, as did Madame Vigée-Lebrun, that after two pregnancies, 'Marie Antoinette remained tall, admirably well made, plump though not too plump. Her arms were superb, her hands small and perfectly formed, and her feet lovely.'[58] Her detractors insisted that she was worried about ageing and had asked Madame Campan to consult Mademoiselle Guimard, a dancer at the Opera, about her methods for erasing signs of age. The perfumer heard the gossip and slipped some *eau de beauté* or *eau favorite* into one of his deliveries, though he believed, like Madame Vigée-Lebrun, that all Marie Antoinette needed was 'a bit of rouge to bring out the translucence of her skin, that was without shadows'. Blending *eau de vie*, benzoin and Brazil wood with an equal portion of rock alum, he produced a liquid that, when lightly rubbed on the cheeks, made it difficult to discern if the person had applied rouge, or if this was her natural colouring.[59]

Adopting Marie Antoinette's style, the women of France began to wear crowns of artificial flowers and to cover their clothes and hats with garlands. Everywhere one saw only nymphs adorned with these false and costly imitations of nature. Solid-coloured or striped skirts were decked with sweet peas, head wear with lilac spangles, fichus were embroidered with jasmine garlands. Flowers reigned everywhere. The Salon de la Méridienne, redecorated in 1781, resembled a hymn to feminine beauty and an invitation to coquetry. Floral garlands complemented the Rousseau brothers' sculptures, and cascades of roses bordered the panelling. This salon was the room where the Queen usually received her purveyors. The inspiration was that of an idealized countryside, where ladies would never soil their little clogs with horse manure. Fargeon also named his perfumes in keeping with the spirits of the times, 'buttercup' or 'flowered prairie' or 'spring bouquet'. Perfecting these supposedly natural scents became more and more complex, and providing the *eaux surfines* with all their power of illusion demanded a long process of preparation. The ladies, whose ambition was to resemble wild flowers, had ceased to paint their faces like bisque dolls, but their simplicity was in fact the height of artifice. Colours took on the most bizarre and outlandish names – 'caca dauphin' for yellowish green, 'Paris mud' or 'goose shit' for iridescent brown, 'Opera fire' for an incandescent red, in allusion to the fire at the Opera at Palais Royal on 15 June 1781, and even, in a rather strange metaphor, 'entrails of little master'.

Fargeon usually saw Marie Antoinette very briefly at her *toilette*, but one day she had him summoned to the Trianon. He was enchanted to discover the little footpaths and the flowered lawns of this small paradise. A valet dressed as a shepherd said he was expected and took him to the Queen, who was walking alone in a lane, wearing a dress of lawn tied with a wide ribbon sash. As he bowed, he breathed in a perfume of iris and recognized with a rush of pleasure that it was one of his creations.

Marie Antoinette had a unique way of walking that made her literally and figuratively heads above any other woman in France. She carried her head high, with a majesty that made her stand out as the sovereign in the midst of the entire Court, yet this regal air in no way spoiled her look of gentleness and kindness, her combination of grace and nobility.[60] In the Trianon, however, her walk was different, more relaxed but nonetheless inspiring no loss of respect.[61]

The Queen thanked Fargeon, as though she were not his sovereign but somehow indebted to him. She explained that she wanted him to capture the essence of the Trianon in a perfume so that she could carry it wherever she went. She remarked that she loved roses and that the tuberose had a strange power over her, which surprised him, since, as scents go, it was anything but light. As she spoke, he looked furtively at her complexion, to retain what was special about it. Her skin was so transparent that it did not take on any shadow. No colour existed to paint this freshness, these tones so delicate that belonged only to this lovely face.[62]

The Queen had him sit next to her on a moss-covered bench facing the Belvedere. She talked about the decoration of this pavilion, which she wished to dedicate entirely to flowers and perfumes. Before bidding him goodbye, she asked him to prepare a toilet water destined for a man who was very elegant but had nothing of the dandy about him, someone as 'virile as one can possibly be'.

The perfume Marie Antoinette ordered posed some difficult problems, for it had to evoke both the tranquillity of the Trianon and the formal, public side of the Queen. Their intimate interview had been brief, but Fargeon had strongly sensed that the sovereign was nothing like the caricature drawn of her. She appeared to be kind and gentle, majestic without the least haughtiness, impulsive and perhaps imprudent but not, as her brother said, a 'head to the wind'. Her simplicity also seemed to be genuine. Indeed, she was known for her plain habits, including in matters of diet. At breakfast she had coffee or chocolate, she ate only white meat and drank only water from the springs of Ville d'Avray, the only one she found digestible. Her supper was broth and a wing of fowl, along with a glass of water in which she dunked little biscuits.

Fargeon composed the *parfum du Trianon* as one would a
piece of music, thinking that the woman who would wear it
loved to sing, to play the harpsichord and the harp, and was
a patron of Glück and had heard his *Orphée*, whose novelty
she admired. The dominant note should be pure rose, at
once seductive and protecting, gathering around it the most
precious and noble essences. He thought of the petals of
orange blossom, white, thick, rich in scent and in freshness,
a rising zephyr like the kiss of a child. To this preparation he
added a bit of *esprit de fleurs d'orange* whose freshness makes
the skin tingle and the waft of whose smell inspires a voluptuous drunkenness. He toned it down with a peaceful touch of
esprit de lavande and added essential oils of citron and bergamot, obtained by pressing them. The Queen knew these well
and would appreciate their familiar touch. The final trace was
galbanum, an oily substance, ductile as wax, of which he liked
to add a few drops to lend a boost of green like a little crack of
the whip between the perfume's main notes of the head and
the heart. That was what he felt, very clearly, every time he
broke the green stem and liberated this powerful note. It was
a reminder that the Queen had broken the codes of etiquette
with her free spirit and dared to go beyond the confines of
courtly routine.

The iris immediately asserted itself. This flower, named for
a messenger of Zeus in Greek mythology, gave a 'miraculous
dust'. Its lofty bearing reminded one of the Queen around
whom the iris already created a halo of scent. Its secret perfume
spread a unique warmth, at once powerful and controlled,
that lent an absolute grace. Jean-Louis Fargeon had already
used it to perfume the Queen's gloves and hair powder by
using the rhizomes that liberated a precious essence, as well
as the flower's powder, that had a distinctive note. He had
noticed that one could give a composition the scent of violet
by using iris. The rose's great rival in the Queen's favour, the
violet, suddenly stood out in the essential oil. It was a singular flower that masqueraded as shy, but whose powerful
and distinctive perfume had nothing of the reserved about

it, contrasting with the image of modesty of a flower that preferred the shade. The violet was the very essence of the fresh and spontaneous Dauphine who, once she had become Queen, had to learn to hide her true nature and call upon all her powers of cunning. It was also said that the fragrance of violets stirred the memory of old loves. That is why Fargeon wanted to add them to his composition, not only by means of the iris, but also using their own leaves, from which he took the perfume through the essential oils. Then he added just a touch of jonquil, wild, bewitching and demanding, this apparently fragile flower that lit up the Trianon and exuded a pure perfume of contrasting tones, an opulent and intimate chord, enough to make one light-headed.

At this point, the three white queens of the night, jasmine, lily and tuberose, intervened. He had to grant them the discreet means of their triumph, sublimate them without betraying them, refine them and present them in all their nuances. He loved the jasmine for its elegantly curved leaves and its delicate petals of porcelain white. The flower's fragility contrasted with the startling power of its perfume which, applied to the skin, declared its freshness and its sumptuousness. The flower of Grasse par excellence, the jasmine had immense range, but, like the Queen of France, it knew how to make itself loved without ever having to give itself completely. Fargeon thought of the lily and the sweet liquid extracted from it that gave off the troubling sensuality of a radiant perfume. The silken strength of its white petals revealed a delicious, almost aqueous coolness, emphasized by a subtle hint of green, barely open leaves. The royal emblem had a brilliant spirit, but the perfumer realized that its heavenly vapour could also be fatal to the composition he was perfecting. It would be representative of the monarchy, not of the true personality of the Queen, and it would be better not to employ it. In any case, he was thinking of the tuberose, with its long stem, soaring majestically towards the sky. Grasse was the abundant source of an excellent type whose white, thick, velvety petals exuded an enchanting, sweet, even erotic perfume. Fargeon had observed that the tuberose had the power to discourage anxiety and stimulate desire. He added just a pinch, for the Queen loved the flower in its natural state but was wary of the rapidly obsessional power of a scent that was halfway between honey and venom. Did the tuberose have a whiff of what Marie Antoinette most loathed, the destructive corruption of the soul?

Finally the perfumer had to reinforce the depth and perfect the harmony of his preparation. Vanilla would lend a warm and delicious touch, soft and velvety, redolent of Marie Antoinette's childhood and her fondness for Viennese pastries, a gourmet hint of sweetness and gentleness. Cedar and sandalwood would add the note of the wooded lanes of the Trianon. Amber and musk would overlay the entire composition with a sensual, animal fervour, and a pinch of benzoin would add warmth and tenacity to the whole.

The composition destined for the 'elegant and virile' man presented a much less difficult problem. Bergamot, jasmine and oak moss on a foundation of a hint of leather, a noble and refined scent, would be perfect. The lingering fragrance of the man who wore this would be like the seal of a secret love.

Fargeon brought his precious package to the Trianon himself and asked Bonnefoy du Plan to give it to the Queen personally. A few days later, he learned that she had been entirely satisfied with his perfume.

III

The Basic Tenor
1782–1794

Nature gave you beauty, like a morning rose
But she would pluck you, like a rose in the evening.
ANTOINE LE CAMUS, physician,
author of *L'Art de conserver la beauté*

∂ Reducing the Queen's spending ∝

The success of the *parfum du Trianon* gave Fargeon the right
to be present at the *grande toilette* of the Queen. He stood
discreetly by the door, waiting to be noticed, while the Queen
talked with her ladies and her closest friends. Sometimes
Marie Antoinette would gesture for him to come closer and
greet him graciously, asking after his wife and children before
requesting his professional advice. Back in the rue du Roule,
however, the atmosphere was always rife with criticism for
'Madame Deficit', as she was now nicknamed. Victoire felt
her husband did not express sufficient indignation at these
remarks, but their political discussions ended there.

The perfumer was at the high point of his career. This was
the century of coquetry, illuminated by the light of science.
Every morning, aristocratic women received nobles, poets,
philosophers, court clergy and parasites in their temples of
finery, surrounded by ewers, boxes of make-up and beauty
spots, toilet kits, cases, small bottles in the bizarre shapes
of birds, monkeys or dogs, all of which served to preserve
their beauty. The *toilette* had a social function which the witty
Marquis Caraccioli, ambassador to Naples, described better
than anyone:

This is where gallantry, as if enthroned, receives its love notes, answers them with others, introduces love and sends it away, caresses it and scolds it, irritates it and ends it; this is where the marquis, armed with clever words, competes with the knight for the conquest of the beautiful widow or the divine countess; this is where parrots, canaries and dogs wander in one after another, to be admired and kissed; this is where trembling chambermaids are dismissed, brought back, and always scolded, and where a poor coiffeur, his comb in the air for the past two hours, waits for a weather vane head to at last hold still so that he can set just one curl, on the run. And it is ultimately in a chamber during the *toilette* that a priest seeking support for a foundation tells spicy anecdotes, plays the jester, and joins with the doctor to compliment Madame on her magnificent complexion, her brilliant health, her many graceful attributes and her well-turned mind.[63]

The Queen's *toilettes* were increasingly expensive and, as acerbic criticism rose, Versailles made a great if largely ineffective effort to reduce expenditure. In 1781 the Comtesse d'Ossun, niece of the Duc de Choiseul and sister of the Duc de Guiche, had succeeded the Duchesse de Mailly as *dame d'atours*, the third most important position in the Queen's Household. She was thirty years old and had great common sense, frowned upon waste but not upon pleasure, was much appreciated by Marie Antoinette and thus ideal for this difficult position. Disappointed by the cupidity of Madame de Polignac's entourage and exasperated by Madame de Lamballe's incessant caprices, the Queen admired the selflessness of this woman of limited means whom she had to force to accept a salary. She was perhaps not as witty as her close friends, but she asked for nothing, either for herself or for her relatives, and made it her business to find simple and reasonably priced pleasures for her mistress. She organized little balls and concerts where singers who were currently in style appeared, at a time when Marie Antoinette was reluctant to attend the Opera for fear of encountering a public that might treat her coldly or with hostility. When she took over the job, the Comtesse d'Ossun asked to be apprised of the exact state of things. The Secretary of the Wardrobe wrote a lengthy report to inform her of how the service functioned, and she found many irregularities in it. After having spoken with each of the purveyors, she decided to put the accounts in order. The following year, 1782, was thus the year of the 'Wardrobe reform'.

The principal expenses did not concern perfumery, and Fargeon discovered that, the previous year, his products had accounted for less than a tenth of the 110,000 livres spent on 'fashions and outfits'. Despite all her good resolutions, Marie Antoinette was incapable of resisting the temptation of a new outfit and, ironically, her love of simplicity was becoming ruinous. To put an end to her extravagances, it was decided to 'fix the number of outfits and dresses necessary per season and per year and to restrain the quantity of accessories and jewellery that went with them'.[64] The merchants of fashionable apparel were forbidden to bring their products directly to the Queen without an initial inspection by the *dame d'atours* who would never fail to put a brake on their enterprise. They had to declare their prices before handing over the bills, which they were sure to be late in doing, taking advantage of the fact that their order had been overlooked to consequently scandalously inflate the price.

Despite all her efforts, the Comtesse d'Ossun could not stop the flood single-handed. She was obliged to write to the Comptroller General on 16 May 1783, 'I am honoured to address to you, Monsieur, the general state of expenses for the wardrobe of the Queen during the year 1782. These far surpass what I would have wished … I am in a position to hope that the current year will prove less costly.'[65] Nothing, however, would be possible without restricting the extravagance of the Queen's favoured milliner, Rose Bertin. The other purveyors also became subject to increasingly strict control. The patroness of Fargeon's early days, the Princesse de Guéménée, did not escape financial difficulties either, for her husband had suffered a staggering bankruptcy of twenty-eight million livres, and the scandal forced the Princess to resign from her post as governess of the Children of France. She was replaced by Madame de Polignac, who encouraged recklessness and squandering.

❧ Marie Antoinette vilified ❧

Increasingly, everything the Queen did was disparaged, and her pastoral refuge at the Trianon passed for a den of vice. She began to spend more time there and every year added to her ideas for improving it. A Temple of Love with a round colonnade holding a Bouchardon-sculpted Cupid captive rose in the middle of an island planted with paradise apple trees, snowball rose bushes, and lilacs; a grotto was sculpted in rock, shadowed by pines, thuja conifers and larches. Richard Mique designed a dolls' village, a hamlet with nine little thatched-roof cottages. The Queen could at last play farmer's wife, watch the cows being milked, and churn the butter in a marble dairy. Other innocent amusements inflamed the gossip and antipathy. She would appear on stage in her little theatre at the Trianon, playing Colette in *Le Devin du village* by Jean-Jacques Rousseau, or Rosine in Beaumarchais's *The Barber of Seville*.

Such follies enraged popular opinion. The days of an adoring public had long since passed and the thousands of 'lovers' the Duc de Brissac had presented to the Dauphine in 1773 had disappeared. Even in 1779 Parisians had stayed away from the ceremony of *relevailles* (getting up for the first time after childbirth) that followed the birth of her daughter. Marie Antoinette became the target of ferocious lampoons and songs, yet she continued to attribute them simply to the French nature: 'They are rather thoughtless in character, but not bad; pens and tongues say many things that do not come from the heart,' she wrote to her mother, the Empress. Like the charming shepherdesses and flute-playing shepherd boys Marie Antoinette had installed in her Trianon, her subjects were creatures of fiction to her. And yet, paradoxically, she had a dozen poor families installed in the Trianon and paid all their expenses from her own pocket.

෨෧෫

Even in her own chateaux and among her closest courtiers, the Queen was surrounded by enemies. The aunts in their salons of Bellevue welcomed every nasty rumour. At the Palais-Royal, the home of the Orléans family, they dreamed of a political order imbued with the ideas of the Enlightenment and inspired by Jean-Jacques Rousseau. Officers returning from the American War of Independence sang the praises of a country where liberty and equality had abolished classes and privileges. In the eyes of many, the Queen was secretly direct-ing public affairs to favour Austria, her true country. To this end, she nominated incompetent ministers and gave damag-ing advice to a country she was simultaneously pushing toward bankruptcy with her squandering. She was criticized as a 'carefree spendthrift, the eternally frivolous chatelaine of the Trianon, who absurdly sacrifices the love and the well being of twenty million men to an arrogant clique of twenty gentlemen and ladies'.[66]

Many accused her of adultery because of her fondness for Comte Axel de Fersen. She had met the handsome officer upon his arrival in Paris in 1775. He had everything the King of France did not: great presence, beauty and passion. Already, in April 1779, the ambassador of Sweden had written to his King, 'The young Comte de Fersen finds such favour with the Queen that several people have taken umbrage. I admit that I cannot keep from believing she has a weakness for him, and I have seen indications that are too obvious to be in doubt.' De Fersen refused to further compromise the Queen and went to fight with Rochambeau in America to escape the rumours, but when he returned to Paris he was every bit as smitten. His sister was the only one he confided in: 'I cannot belong to the only person I want to belong to, the only one who truly loves me.'[67] In turn, Marie Antoinette gave him a seal stamped with the motto, *'Tutto a te me guida'* (everything leads me to you).

She would one day describe him as her 'only true friend'. From 1785 to 1787 de Fersen divided his time between Versailles and Maubeuge, where he was quartered with the regiment granted him by the King, whom snide remarks described as the complacent cuckold. He never married, and he tried to serve the Queen to the end, when he would risk his life and honour in an attempt to save her.

❧❦

Despite his loyalty to the Queen, Fargeon began to foster an interest in the ideas of equality and fraternity emerging in France at the time. He discussed them in letters with his brother, Joseph Jacques Mathieu, member of the Masonic lodge La nouvelle amitié of Grasse. Together they condemned a corrupt power and an archaic society and sang the praises of the democracy of antiquity.

Versailles remained seemingly oblivious to the simmering discontent. Despite the good intentions of the Comtesse d'Ossun, the accounts of the wardrobe reached the unprecedented summit of 258,000 livres in 1785. In the hands of Rose Bertin, austerity cost a fortune. Simple and light fabrics were all the rage. This fashion had originated in Bordeaux, introduced by the creoles of Santo Domingo who wore only heavy cotton, lawn and calico. On Bertin's advice, the Queen developed a passion for white muslin and pleated taffeta. Madame Vigée-Lebrun painted her portrait, and malevolent visitors to the Salon 'did not fail to say that the Queen had been painted in her chemise'.[68]

On 27 March 1785 Marie Antoinette was delivered of a second son, Louis Charles, Duc de Normandie, the future Louis XVII. This lovely child, described by the Queen in letters to her mother as 'solid as the son of a peasant', did not win her back the affection of the French people and she continued to provide her enemies with ammunition. Monsieur de Calonne was far too fawning a minister not to open his coffers wide to her every whim, and Rose Bertin obstinately refused to be controlled. To the horror of the accountants of Versailles, she demanded extraordinary prices, according to the Comtesse d'Adhémar, 'without providing any detailed description, for every single costume or ensemble'.

The disastrous Affair of the Diamond Necklace, in which Marie Antoinette would seem to have been impersonated as part of a plot to rob the jeweller Boehmer of the said gemstones, smeared the Queen and the monarchy with a scandal from which they would never truly recover. Madame Campan described the affair as, 'A hidden intrigue, put together by swindlers, in the shadow of a corrupt society'.[69] The trial of Cardinal Rohan, who had been caught up in the deception, opened on 15 August 1785, with the entire Court in attendance. The Queen demanded that Cardinal Rohan be judged and that the truth be established, but the gallant prelate passed for a victim, and the pamphleteers had a field day. The adventuress Jeanne de La Motte, who had orchestrated the whole scheme, was sentenced to life imprisonment and would be whipped and branded before her incarceration. Mademoiselle d'Oliva, who had impersonated Marie Antoinette in the role of the Queen who coveted the gift of an expensive necklace from the jeweller Boehmer, was exonerated. The news of the Cardinal's acquittal brought a round of applause, as spontaneous as it was insulting to the Queen, who burst into sobs when the verdict was announced.

She was vilified in the street. A quatrain of dialogue between the Queen and the impersonator made the rounds and was for a time very popular:

Marie Antoinette:
You, little grisette, it suits you so well
To play my role as Queen!

Mademoiselle d'Oliva:
And why not, my sovereign?
You so often play mine!

Despite her lucrative service to the Queen, Rose Bertin declared bankruptcy in January 1787 and the Baronne d'Oberkirch, who had never pardoned her earlier smugness, said with irony, 'La Bertin, so proud, so haughty, ever so insolent ... has just declared bankruptcy. It is true that this is no plebian bankruptcy, but that of a great lady. Two million, that's something else for someone in the rag trade!' Others insisted the said bankruptcy was feigned, simply a means of forcing the Court to pay its outstanding debts, beginning with the two million owed by a 'certain individual'. In fact, in the years that followed, Rose Bertin was apparently so little ruined that she made some important investments in Parisian real estate.[70]

Fargeon admired her talent but took her for a poor businesswoman and, like his colleagues, he blamed her for taking such a large portion of the Queen's expenditure. He was neither surprised nor saddened by her downfall. His business was doing well, he was established at Court and engaged in considerable commerce abroad, especially with England and America. Only one of his creations was threatened, for Madame Vigée-Lebrun was trying to influence the Queen to stop using powder. 'Painting the Queen,' she wrote, 'I begged her not to wear powder any more and to part the hair on her forehead.' 'I will be the last one to follow this style,' laughed the Queen. 'I wouldn't want people to say that I thought of it to hide my wide forehead.'[71]

Marie Antoinette, whilst still beautiful, had lost her carefree air forever. Madame Vigée-Lebrun painted her in 1787, surrounded by her children, her expression one of veiled sadness. The Dauphin's health was a source of justified concern, for the following year, as a result of bone tuberculosis, his 'waist moved'. One shoulder was higher than the other, and it seemed abundantly evident that the future King of France would be a hunchback. He suffered from a debilitating fever, and even though he was sent to Meudon, known for its beneficial air, he had lost a good deal of weight. Marie Antoinette had already lost her daughter Princess Marie Sophie at the age of eleven months and, deeply shaken by this ordeal, had written to Madame Elisabeth, 'We weep at the death of my poor little angel. I need all your heart to console my own.' A tender and attentive mother, she was no longer concerned with dictating fashion or being the queen of the clotheshorses.

ॐ The 'perfume factory' of Suresnes ॐ

The boutique at the rue du Roule had become too cramped and the House of Fargeon had to move its laboratories and workshops to a larger and more adequate establishment. Suresnes had the advantage of proximity to one of the Queen's residences, for she had just bought the Chateau of Saint-Cloud, on the recommendation of the Dauphin's doctors, who maintained that his fragile health demanded a more wholesome air than that of Versailles. The place was also appropriate for the perfume industry. The foothills of Suresnes were by and large devoted to vineyards, but there were also superb fields of a delicate pink flower known as a 'rose of Puteaux' of which Fargeon used great quantities in his compositions.

On their first visit, the Fargeons were enchanted with the gentle tranquillity of the little village and decided to buy several pieces of property there – an indication of the prosperity they enjoyed at the time. One was a beautiful country house in the rue de Seine, whose bill of sale, signed on 31 January 1786, gave the following description:

> two main buildings, one on the river, with access below to several cellars at ground level, and its outbuildings. The entirety bordered on one side by the monks of Religieux de Saint-Germain des Prés, lords of the said Suresnes, and on the other by the house and garden of the Comte de Skelton, residing at the chateau de la Source; at one end to the river Seine, the main pathway between the two and, at the other end, in front, at the so-called rue de Seine or rue des Champs.[72]

The kitchen, the office, the pantry, the dining room, two salons, a chapel, the wardrobe closet and the bathroom were located on the ground floor. Upstairs, most of the twenty-one bedrooms had their own dressing rooms and wardrobe closets. The perfumer had a study for work and, for his leisure, two billiard rooms. And finally, the outbuildings included outhouses, a laundry room, two woodsheds, a greenhouse and an orangery. The stables were installed in the building that faced the main residence and Fargeon rented work space where he and his staff would prepare the perfumes.

There were plenty of people in the surrounding countryside who were willing to work for Fargeon, and the perfume factory rapidly prospered. On 22 August he bought even more buildings to add to his property. Jean-Louis Fargeon was now one of the most prominent men in Suresnes, even more so than the Marquis de Chatenay. He had horses and a carriage, and household servants, and he owned silverware, jewellery and works of art. He actively pursued his research and was intent upon exploiting the latest discoveries, in his own words, in order to 'prepare perfumes the fickle goddess of fashion will grace with her favour now'. Through his letters, his brother kept him abreast of the latest advances in the technique of fixing perfume in fatty matter, which made excellent pomades. It was a speciality of the city of Grasse, and consisted of placing jasmine and tuberose blossom in dishes of pewter or varnished pottery filled with *axonge* (animal fat), which imbibed their odour upon contact. They also ground almonds in a *pâte de Provence*, which sold well in Paris and at Versailles.

Fargeon concentrated his research on the practice of distillation.[73] He manufactured oils of violet, subtle and delicate to capture, of the heady tuberose, of the sensual jasmine and of the wild jonquil. He built an orangery and extracted from its flowers a light oil that never set, called *néroli*. He was fascinated by the work of Denis Papin who, working in the previous century, had endeavoured to use the expansive force of steam. Fargeon tried, by trial and error, to adapt his 'steam machine' to the distilling process, just as it had been used in the textile industry to increase production and reduce prices. The *Mercure de France* had run articles on the progress made in this area, and he liked to imagine that the same thing was possible in the field of perfumery. He installed six boilers, cauldrons and coils of red copper, equipment that was sophisticated for the time. He was convinced that the future lay in 'the application of modern chemistry to this art of perfume'.[74] The Dutch chemist Martinus Van Marum had just written that the origin of odour could be electric and cited that of lightning, which floats in the atmosphere after great summer storms when the air has become less heavy. Antoine Lavoisier's work had also aided immense advances in chemistry.

The orders for the Queen's Household at this time contained more *eaux apaisantes* than *esprits perçants* and beauty elixirs. As the September 1778 *Journal politique ou Gazette des gazettes* mentioned: 'The merchants of Paris are starting to complain that their sales are falling and that the manufacturers have lost confidence in them. This last is unfortunately true. Another equally distressing fact is that many nobles are laying off personnel, some of them up to forty of their staff.' The Queen had set the example: on 16 January 1788 an edict announced a reduction in the operational expenses of her Household of 1,206,600 livres. In June onlookers who witnessed her visit to the Invalides noticed the plainness of her dress. Marie Antoinette perhaps finally sensed the storm was gathering.

Madame d'Adhémar said that one morning she was summoned and found the Queen in the Petit Trianon, wearing a morning négligé, with tears in her eyes. 'I sent for you,' she told me, 'because I must know the truth. Everything is going badly, and I realize that finances are in a terrible state and, what's more, I am accused of ruining the kingdom, to my brother's advantage. It's an incredible falsehood, just as it is untrue that the Duchesse de Polignac dips into the treasury. Monsieur de Calonne is very worried and is talking about calling what is termed an Assembly of Notables. Please tell me what you know about all this.'

Madame d'Adhémar knew very little, but she tried to reassure the Queen concerning a libellous verse by an anonymous author that had been brought to her attention. A violent death was predicted for a king and a queen.

'These threats in rhyme are terrifying!' the Queen cried. 'But to whom do they refer?'

'This can never touch you, Your Majesty,' Madame d'Adhémar replied. 'Incredible things, insane things, are predicted. If all that happens, it will be our great nephews' problem.'

'Heaven help us, I hope you are right,' the Queen answered, 'and yet it is strange that all these things are happening at once.'[75]

Unlucky signs multiplied. One night, when Madame Campan was with her, the Queen was sitting at her dressing table, with four candles lit. One by one, the first three candles went out. 'Unhappiness can make one superstitious,' Marie Antoinette remarked. 'If this fourth candle were to go out like the others, nothing could prevent me from taking it as a sinister omen.' The fourth candle went out.

However, there were many who did not sense the coming storm at the end of the year, 1788. Among the elite, people continued to have fun, to laugh, to enjoy life, as if nothing threatened their existence. Lady Kerry, a client of Fargeon and of Bertin, held a fashionable salon where a raucous gang met twice a week to play at the card games creps and cavagnole. Between two hands, the conversation centred around the latest stylish thing to wear and the importance of rouge or of one's favourite perfume. Fargeon continued to fill orders for his incomparable pot-pourri, whose formula he had perfected in his laboratory in Suresnes.

❧ Republican, above all ❦

The 4 May 1789 marked the first meeting of the Estates General, an assembly made up of representatives from the three different sections of the population. This meeting and its blatant disconnection from the monarchy aided the onset of the French Revolution. Rose Bertin dressed Marie Antoinette for her appearance at the ceremony the following day: 'The

Queen was marvellously turned out, in a simple head band of diamonds, with her lovely heron feather, a violet outfit with a white skirt trimmed with silver sequins. The King wore the Régent on his hat.'[76] For the very last time, the Queen of France and Navarre appeared in all her splendour.

Fargeon was thrilled by the Tennis Court Oath of 20 June. At last he saw the dawning light of a new era. Yet, alongside this, hostility towards the Queen continued apace. One day, in the rue du Roule, Fargeon heard a chorus of drunks sing:

Louis, if you'd like to see
Bastard, cuckold, whore
Look in your mirror,
And at the Queen and the Dauphin.

Victoire was so shocked that one of the shop clerks had to open a bottle of vinegar to keep her from fainting. From that moment on, she only referred to the patriots as 'your scoundrel friends'.

Fargeon, though republican at heart, was a stranger to prejudice and hatred. He did not share the excesses of his camp, and whenever the occasion arose and he could make the remark without risk, he never failed to say that the Queen was by nature kind and generous. Since April 1788 the little Ernestine Lambriquet, orphan of one of Madame Royale's chambermaids, had been raised in the apartments of the governess of the Children of France; she was treated in the same fashion as the Princess and received the same articles from Fargeon's shop. Marie Antoinette had adopted or taken into her protection several children of the poor, and Fargeon asserted that she was nothing like the caricature drawn of her. But he also insisted that the distinction between the woman and the sovereign was important and that every monarchy was, by nature, tyrannical. He believed that man was naturally good, and that only institutions made him bad. The storming of the Bastille on 14 July 1789 appeared to him to be the welcome symbol of the end of royal dictatorship, but he regretted that it had been tarnished with murder. He took part enthusiastically in the National Guard formed by the Parisian bourgeois.

ৰু৽৹৶

On 4 August 1789 the National Assembly abolished the feudal system and the aristocracy relinquished all their privileges. Led by the Duc de Noailles, they declared that they would accept equality of taxation and the abrogation of feudal rights. Spurred on by fear, the clergy offered to abandon the tithe, and the municipal representatives their provincial, municipal and corporate privileges.

Things of luxury disappeared. Gone the extravagant *poufs* and the bonnets *au lever de la Reine* (the moment when the Queen leaves her bed in the morning in the presence of the Court). Now people were wearing Bastille bonnets festooned with the national cockade, or 'citizens' bonnets' in white gauze, of ancient simplicity. Liberty prints of cotton took the place of silk, this time not because of a royal impulse but because splendour was no longer tolerated. Ladies of foreign nobility had already decided it was wise to leave France. The French nobility was not long in following them. At the Queen's insistence, the Duchesse de Polignac fled to Germany. On 8 August the Princesse Louise de Condé was seen in Bonn on her way to Coblenz with the Princesse de Monaco and the Marquise d'Autichamp. On 5 September the Comtesse d'Artois left for Torino. In November the property of the clergy was confiscated as a guarantee for *assignats* (Revolutionary banknotes).

Fargeon's clients scattered to the four corners of Europe. His shop was deserted but the situation was by no means desperate: there were still the foreign clients, and not all the noble clients had emigrated. He realized that he did not have to hide his republican convictions any longer, yet he refused to advertise them, believing it was not the place of a merchant to do so. Others displayed their opinions openly. Milliners sold ribbons the colour of 'blood of fuller's earth'. Rose Bertin, rediscovering her proletarian origins, threw together national cockades that she sold at the exorbitant price of 18 francs apiece. Patriotic ladies wore rings and earrings with a piece of stone from the Bastille set in gold, creating a 'Constitution jewel'. Fargeon did not want to follow the example of the jewellers and concoct a 'liberty pomade' or an *eau de senteur du sans culottes*.

The Marquise de Tourzel, a widow with small children, and nicknamed by the Dauphin 'Madame Sévère', was particularly concerned with Fargeon's well being. Deliveries to the Marquise from the House of Fargeon in August of 1789 included several pairs of white gloves, pairs of *peau de chien* mittens, bottles of lavender, litres of spirits of wine, jars of orange blossom pomade and almond paste pomade, orange blossom powder and scent baskets lined in taffeta perfumed with violet powder or *poudre au cypre*. He also continued to supply the Queen with perfumed fans and he created a *vinaigre radical* or *esprit de Vénus* for her, of which he wrote:

> This liqueur is perhaps the most penetrating I know. It is enough just to remove the stopper of the bottle, wherever it is, to fill an entire apartment with its odour, and if one carries the open bottle next to the nose, it penetrates the brain with such fire that it feels as though the cranium were opening up and separating into two parts. Its perfume is among the most pleasant.[77]

Since the fall of the Bastille, the Queen had known the royal family would be forced to leave Versailles, for successive deputations came to ask the King to come to Paris. She had Madame Campan prepare her jewellery and burned some of her papers in case of an incursion into the chateau. On 5 October her fears were realized when Versailles was invaded by Parisian crowds and the following day rioters forced the King to move to the Tuileries. 'The rabble surrounded His Majesty's carriage and ran in front of it shouting, "We won't be out of bread any more; we have the baker, the baker's wife, and the little baker's boy." In the midst of this troop of cannibals, the heads of the two murdered body guards were brandished high,' wrote Madame Campan, who witnessed the scene. When the King was received at the City Hall, Jean Sylvain

Bailly, President of the National Assembly and one of the early leaders of the Revolution, asked him to sit on a throne, 'while that of his ancestors had just been destroyed'.[78]

The old order had just received a fatal blow. The monarch was no longer respected, and the proof was in the fact that he could be forced to yield. Fargeon did not find this displeasing. The first months of 1790 filled him with hope. On 14 July he took part in the celebration of the Fédération with his section of the National Guard, returning to the Champ de Mars elated. In August Louis XVI reluctantly accepted the Civil Constitution of the Clergy, although many a priest and bishop, following orders from the Pope, refused to take the oath. Fargeon forced his children's private tutor, a priest, to sign it under threat of dismissal. The National Constituent Assembly voted for equitable laws. Fargeon particularly approved of the law proposed by a physician-philanthropist named Dr Ignace Guillotin. 'In cases where the law shall pronounce the death penalty against a defendant, the form of execution shall be the same, whatever the nature of the crime of which he has been convicted. The criminal shall be decapitated with a simple mechanical device.'[79] The Assembly had voted the text into law.

In March 1791 the d'Allarde Law abolished trade guilds, and the Parisian community of glove, purse and belt makers and perfumers, now heavily in debt owing to its contribution towards the construction of a ship for the King's war flotilla, was dissolved. Fargeon applauded the law, but also remembered with sadness the pride he had felt when he was first admitted to the corporation. The abolition of their statute gave perfumers free enterprise, but it was of little value in such uncertain times. It presented no advantage for the workers, and striking still landed one in prison.

❧ The scent of misfortune ❧

Early in June 1791 Fargeon received a disturbing note requesting him to go immediately to the Tuileries, where he should
present himself to the Swiss Guard, who would conduct him
to the place where he would be received. He obeyed at once
and was led through nearly deserted apartments to Marie
Antoinette's study. She greeted him kindly and asked him
what he, as a bourgeois of Paris, thought of events. He had no
desire to declare his republican convictions nor to follow the
example of Léonard and of Mademoiselle Bertin, who prided
themselves on keeping the Queen informed by reporting on
public rumours. He limited himself to saying that his business kept him distanced from politics and to protest that he
felt personally attached to the sovereigns, which, to his mind,
did not constitute an allegiance to the monarchy.

The *parfum du Trianon*, which he had created with such
care, wafted about her, and, astonished, he realized that it had
gone off. In the mysterious alchemy of the scented liquid and
the skin, the bewitching odour of the tuberose had smothered
all the other elements. Yet he knew he had used the dangerous flower sparingly. Something harsh and brutal had made
its way sinuously into the exquisite fragrance, like a premoni-
tion of misfortune.

Fargeon recognized in the air another one of his creations:
the virile fragrance that she had ordered as a gift for a mysterious 'very elegant man'. He had no doubt been in the room
just a few hours ago. He thanked the Queen for her unwaver-
ing confidence in him and, before leaving, told her he had
given Madame Campan the entire contents of her last order,
as well as Madame de Tourzel's. He did not add that he had
found the two lists unusually long, and that he had had great
difficulty gathering all the required items since raw materials
no longer arrived regularly, given the troubles.

The perfumer could not guess the reason for this large
order, for he did not know that the royal family was prepar-
ing for the flight that would end tragically at Varennes. To

save the woman he loved, Axel de Fersen had expended
extraordinary efforts and did not hesitate to take the greatest
risks. Already, in February, he had perfected a plan for escape
to Montmédy, which was preferable to Metz, for it was closer
to Luxembourg. They would avoid passing through Rheims,
where the King had been crowned, in case he was recognized.
A huge berlin, painted bottle green with lemon-yellow wheels
and padded in white Utrecht velvet, was reserved for the trip.
'As early as the month of March,' wrote Madame Campan,
'the Queen began to make preparations for her departure. I
was with her that month, and I executed many of the secret
orders she gave me. It pained me to see her attending to details
that seemed useless and even dangerous to me, and I pointed
out that the Queen of France will find chemises and dresses
everywhere.'[80]

The same was true of perfumes. Marie Antoinette, incor-
rigibly unrealistic, had decided to take them in her vast toilet
kit, completely restocked for the occasion. Like Montesquieu,
she no doubt thought that 'when one has been a woman in
Paris, one can no longer be one elsewhere'. An entire trunk
of her purchases was sent to Brussels, but the kit presented
a more delicate problem, since it was 'enormous, containing everything from a warming pan to a silver platter'.[81] The
Queen thought of the pretext of sending it as a present to her
sister but Madame Campan tried to discourage her, fearing
that 'there were people perceptive enough to guess that this
present was only a pretext to send this article ahead before
her departure'. Great care was taken not to leave any trace
of perfume that would not be to the Princess's taste, but this
precaution did not fool one of the wardrobe servants who
denounced her mistress's true intentions to the Mayor of Paris
on 21 May. 'Her Majesty was too attached to this piece to part
with it,' she added, 'and she had often remarked that it would
be very useful for a trip.'[82]

In order to fill the crystal bottles, the powder boxes and
unguent jars of her kit, Marie Antoinette had placed orders
for innumerable articles with her various purveyors. Besides

the *parfum du Trianon*, Fargeon had his famous *poudre à la Fargeon*, jars of pomade, a few bottles of *eau de lavande, eau céleste* and *eau souveraine*, which the Queen liked to rub on her temples, delivered to her. Fearing the strenuousness of the voyage, she had also added *eau de fleur d'orange* and *esprit de lavande*, known for their soothing qualities, as well as smelling salts and sachets of *bain de modestie*. And she had not forgotten *essence de la bergamote*, nor heliotrope and lemon pomades, nor various cosmetic lotions. She had not told Fargeon that she also much appreciated his competitor Jean-Louis Houbigant's *esprits perçants* and his *crème de rose aux limaçons*.

An extraordinary accumulation of blunders preceded and accompanied the flight to Varennes, but Marie Antoinette's coquettishness also influenced things adversely. She could not conceive of going without her coiffeur, so Léonard was informed. He was to bring the coffer carrying the Queen's diamonds and to alert the horse relays of the approach of the fugitives. On 20 June the huge and not very discreet berlin carried off the royal couple, alias Monsieur Durand and Madame Rochet, and their two children, as well as Madame Elisabeth and Madame de Tourzel. In fact the departure of the royal family was an open secret, perhaps tolerated by the masters of France because they expected to extract political advantage from it. 'Monsieur Durand' was recognized several times over before the master of the posts, Jean-Baptiste Drouet, turned him in. The trusted hairdresser managed – through treason or foolishness – to tell the dragoons who had come to protect the King that there had been a counter-order, and so they left their post. When the officers arrived from Paris, carrying the Assembly's order to 'have all individuals of the royal family arrested', Louis XVI murmured, 'There is no longer a king in France.'[83] The Queen, in a useless and provocative gesture, threw the decree to the ground. Their return was dreadful. In the heat and dust, the berlin had become a prison on wheels, escorted by armed troops and booed at by a furious populace. Upon arrival, the Queen, whose hair had turned white from the ordeal, dictated a note for Madame

Campan: 'I am writing to you from my bath, in which I have just immersed myself to restore at least my physical strength. I cannot say anything about the state of my soul; we exist, that is all.' She owed this small comfort to the art of her favourite perfumer.

Everyone who was suspected of having aided the King was persecuted. The *dame d'atours*, Madame d'Ossun, arrested on the spot, gave her interrogators this fine and proud reply: 'I was not in on the secret. If I had been, I would not be here, I would have preceded the Queen. If one thing makes me angry, it is that the Queen did not warn me of all this.'[84] Fargeon, too, had good reason to worry, since the berlin had been fairly bursting with products from his boutique. Would he be taken for an accomplice in an undertaking that he, as a good patriot, viewed as an unpardonable crime against the nation?

ॐ∞

The flight to Varennes cemented the death of the monarchy. The National Assembly, attempting to avert the abdication of the King and the establishment of a Republic, forced Louis XVI to swear an oath to the constitution. From that moment on, his powers were negated and his position as King was in name only. On 3 September the Constitution of 1791 was proclaimed. Abroad, the threat of war from countries loyal to the King loomed, and at home France was weakened by poverty and discontent. On 20 April 1792 France declared war on Austria. A few weeks later, Prussia joined with Austria, heralding the beginning of the French Revolutionary Wars.

Fargeon stayed at home on 20 June 1792, when a furious crowd barged into the Tuileries. Carried high above their heads was a guillotine with the inscription 'For the tyrant' and a gallows with the effigy of a woman hanging from it, inscribed 'For Antoinette'. Louis XVI allowed a red Phrygian bonnet to be placed upon his head. In the rue du Roule, Fargeon's clients were horrified. The butcher Legendre had addressed the King as 'Monsieur'. 'You are a perfidious person,' he had continued, 'you have always deceived us, and you will deceive us again!' It was said that Marie Antoinette acted with courage and dignity when a woman in the crowd insulted her. The Queen, who was separated from the furious crowd only by a table, asked the woman if she had done her some personal harm. 'None,' replied the woman, 'but you have caused the downfall of the nation.' 'You have been misled,' the Queen answered. 'I married the King of France and I am the mother of the Dauphin. I am French, and I shall never again see my native land. I can only be happy or unhappy in France, and I was happy when you loved me.' The woman burst into tears. 'Ah, Madame, pardon me. I did not know you and I see that you are good.'[85]

On 25 July the Brunswick Manifesto, in which the general in command of the Austro-Prussian army threatened France with invasion if they refused to obey the King, set off the powder keg. Paris was enraged and the little army of the *fédérés*, consisting of 500 troops from Marseilles and 300 from Brittany, readied themselved to fuel the insurrection. Fargeon had followed the general movement, but was not among those who launched the second assault on the Tuileries, this 'den of nobles and priests'. On 10 August, in a 'deep volcano of fury',[86] the assailants massacred the Swiss Guard, whom the King had ordered to hold their fire to spare the blood of his people. Some of the Queen's attendants were momentarily threatened but were released with a contemptuous 'Rascals, the nation has spared you!' The King and his family were ordered to place themselves under the protection of the Assembly. On 13 August they were transferred to the Temple.

❧ The last deliveries ❧

No one dared declare himself purveyor to the Crown any longer but Fargeon continued to serve the Queen in prison.[87] He learned that she constantly used his *vinaigrettes* of *eaux revigorantes* to help her endure the ordeal, and that she used a good deal of *eau de vie de lavande* to calm her anxiety, along with orange blossom pomades and hand cream. Fargeon placed a little bottle of *parfum du Trianon* among the other scents, as a reminder of happier days. When he went to be paid for this delivery, a sans culottes laughed in his face.

Rose Bertin had fled to Coblenz, where her former clients were waiting for her. It was said that she had finally heeded the warnings of the Queen, who feared for her faithful milliner. Bertin's departure sounded the death knell for luxury and frivolity, and one paper wrote, 'Mademoiselle Bertin is leaving, there will be no one left in Paris but the kindling makers.' The best informed knew that the Queen had told her milliner, on the occasion of one of her last deliveries to the Tuileries, 'Last night I dreamt of you, dear Rose. It seemed you were bringing me lots of ribbons of all different colours, and I chose several, but as soon as I took them in my hands, they turned black.'[88]

The climate in Paris was increasingly volatile. Sans culottes searched every house and filled the prisons with suspects. Jean-Louis Fargeon went out as little as possible, for, even though he was a patriot, his manner of dress and speech suggested otherwise. On 17 August Dr Guillotin's machine had been inaugurated to execute Laporte, steward of the civil list of Louis XVI, and Anglemont, 'royalist agent'. It was decided that the guillotine would be set up permanently from now on. At the beginning of September, on the pretext of liquidating the enemies within, bands of cutthroats descended upon the prisons that were full to overflowing with suspects. Marseilles troops and *fédérés* killed several bishops and 120 priests in a massacre that lasted two hours at Carmes prison. Those of the Swiss Guard who had been spared on 10 August were murdered at the Prison de l'Abbaye. No one was spared, neither the women interned in Salpêtrière, nor the children at Bicêtre. The Princesse de Lamballe was dragged out of the Prison de la Force and killed. Having taken refuge in Torino, she had returned to France as soon as she heard that her friend the Queen was in danger. Her head, stuck on a pike, was carried to the Temple so that Marie Antoinette could see it from her window. 'People,' Jean-Nicolas Billaud-Varenne, one of the most violent proponents of the Revolution, proclaimed, 'you slay your enemies, you do your duty!' On 21 September 1792 the National Convention decreed that the monarchy had been abolished in France. 'Kings,' proclaimed the Abbé Grégoire, 'are to the moral order what monsters are to the physical order.'[89] He was applauded with cries of 'Vive la nation! Vive la liberté!' All public acts had to be dated from the first year of the Republic and the State seal bore the words 'République de France'.

Fargeon thought of his father, as he had when privileges were abolished. No doubt he would have liked to have seen the Republic take the place of royalty, but would this have been the way the reader of the philosophers envisaged a new era? He felt his faith in the Revolution wavering. Despite his own precarious position as a former purveyor to the King and Queen, the society of enlightened and well-meaning equals he and his father had dreamed of had given way to blood-thirsty fanatics. Fargeon never again set foot in his section of the National Guard with any enthusiasm. And he was not alone. 'In a section consisting of three to four thousand citizens, only twenty-five have formed the assembly,' declared a December 1792 report. That same month, Marat wrote in his blistering attack, 'The assemblies are deserted, due to disgust and ennui.'[90]

Fargeon knew nothing of the daily existence of the prisoners at the Temple, unaware that jailers in red caps ill-treated the royal family, who endured all with stoicism. An erstwhile Capuchin *ci-devant*, the town official Mathieu, had told Louis XVI, 'The country is in danger. We know that we, our wives, and our children will perish, but the people will be avenged, and you will die before we will.'[91]

❧ The pungent odour of blood ❧

Fargeon subscribed to the largest possible number of news sheets and journals, wanting to be informed about the evolution of events. The articles he read were calls for murder. Chemistry had given him a taste for the rigorous and the exact, and the approximations of politics bothered him. Louis XVI, a monarch who was moderate to the point of spinelessness, who had allowed his supporters to be massacred rather than ordering them to open fire upon his enemies, who had abolished torture, including the gruesome ordeal of the wheel, was presented as a bloodthirsty tiger, a modern Nero.

When the 'iron closet', a secret cache in the Tuileries, designed to hide compromising correspondence with the enemies of France, was discovered, Fargeon realized that the King was doomed. The National Convention acted as a tribunal. On 11 December the Mayor of Paris, Chambon, accompanied by the City Prosecutor, Chaumette, came to read the sovereign the following decree: 'Louis Capet will be tried at the bar of the National Assembly'.

The conclusion of the King's plea was read by his defence counsel, Monsieur de Sèze: 'Frenchmen, the revolution that inspires you has developed great virtues in you, but beware that it has not weakened the sentiment of humanity in your souls.'[92]

On the morning of 21 January 1793 the rolling of the drums and the sound of the cannon announced to Marie Antoinette that Louis XVI had just been executed. She wept and then knelt before her son Louis, the seventeenth of his name, King of France and Navarre. The 'widow Capet' was authorized to order 'dresses for deep mourning, shoes of polished leather, petticoats of *hystaly*, and even a fan of black taffeta'.[93] At thirty-seven, Marie Antoinette's legendary beauty had faded. She was an ageing woman in unstable health and subject to frequent convulsions.

The boutique was all but deserted, and Fargeon brought out his claims. The bills dating through the last two years of the reign of Louis XVI were in the hands of Citizen Henry, the liquidator of the civil list, who signed an authorization for payment without a word and with an expression of profound disgust. The receipt read, 'remuneration by the Republic for provisions for Capet, widow of the last tyrant of the French'.[94]

Fargeon consulted the registers where Victoire had recorded the royal orders with her usual meticulousness. The first dated from 1775 and they spread over seventeen years. He made a huge fire and spent several hours burning these now compromising documents. All the suppliers of Versailles were undoubtedly doing the same thing. Rose Bertin had returned from exile. Taken for an émigré, her property had been confiscated but she was able to see the Queen one last time when she delivered a few things to her.

The 3 July 1793 marked perhaps the most tragic day of Marie Antoinette's life. On that day, her son was snatched from her. Among the group of men who invaded the prison cell to kidnap the boy, it pained Fargeon to read the names of a stone cutter, a painter, an attorney, a 'reader and secretary' – and one of his colleagues.

If he had been able to visit her, it would have been difficult for him to recognize the Queen. Her face, whose delicate complexion he had once admired, had become that of an old woman. On 2 August, when she was led to the Conciergerie which, she knew, was the antechamber of death, she apparently sighed, 'Nothing can hurt me now.' She was treated with extreme harshness. She slept on a wooden bed with a straw mattress covered with a dirty blanket. A young servant named Rosalie tried to make the last days of the Queen of France easier. The heat was suffocating and she had little to wear. She was finally granted a few chemises, two pairs of black silk stockings and some shoes. Rosalie obtained a swan's down powder puff for her, along with some powder and a bottle of scented water for her teeth. Her last luxury was to drink Ville d'Avray mineral water, the only water she could stand at Versailles.

Marie Antoinette would get up at seven, put on her peignoir and slippers, and 'part her hair over the forehead after having dusted it with a bit of scented powder'.[95] Even this was too much, and her *vinaigrettes* were confiscated, along with her powder and the swan's down puff, but the gendarmes knew she loved flowers and brought her carnations and tuberoses. The watch that the King had given her was taken away, as well as the three rings, each mounted with two diamond solitaires, that she constantly turned on her fingers to chase boredom and anxiety. All she had left were two patched gowns, one white and the other black, and a little mirror that Rosalie had bought on the quais for 25 sous of *assignats*. She was enchanted with its red border painted with Chinese motifs. The woman who had once owned the most beautiful travel toilet kit in the world arranged her rags in a cardboard box.

The terrible Law of Suspects, which sanctioned the trial and execution of those merely suspected of treason against the Republic, was passed on 17 September 1793. A month later, Marie Antoinette mounted the scaffold. Fargeon read her sentence in the *Moniteur*: 'In hearing her sentence, she did not show any reaction, and she left the courtroom without a word, without any speech, either to the judges or to the public.' The perfumer no longer sought to distinguish between the Queen and the woman, to condemn one and to pity the other, as he once had. He skimmed over the funeral oration vomited by the leader of the Commune of Paris, Jacques Rene Hébert, in the *Père Duchesne* with disgust:

> I saw the head of the female veto fall into the sack! Damned if I wouldn't love to tell you of the satisfaction of the sans culottes when the archduchess crossed Paris in the coach with six doors. Her cursed head is finally separated from her tart's neck. The air echoed with cries of 'Vive la République!'

While Victoire wept, Fargeon thought back to the young Dauphine, resplendent with beauty, grace and majesty. He recalled his last visit to the Tuileries and how the *parfum du Trianon* had turned, foretelling tragedy with its corrupted scent. He remembered Marie Antoinette saying the tuberose had a strange power over her. Why did she so love a flower that resembled her so little and that, when it decayed, exuded a smell of decomposing flesh? He thought of Rousseau's words: 'Olfaction is the sense of the imagination.' Had the Queen anticipated her fate?

☞☜

After Marie Antoinette's death, Fargeon retreated to his home and remained there for a long time. He did not miss the old regime, but the Revolution had soiled itself with too many crimes for anything good to come of it from now on. The Terror raged, and every day brought the news of still more of his clients who had mounted the scaffolding after spurious trials. Despite his convictions, Fargeon was more upset by Madame Du Barry's end, on 9 November, than by the execution the previous day of the republican Madame Roland. After Louis XV's death, Du Barry had completed eighteen months of forced penitence at the Abbey of Pont aux Dames, returning to find the life she was used to, along with new love affairs. But she paid dearly for her past. 'Citizen jurors,' the public prosecutor cried,

> you have rendered your verdict on the plotting of the spouse of the last tyrant of the French, today it is time to judge the conspiracies of the courtesan of his predecessor. Before you stands this famous Laïs, notorious for her moral dissoluteness, the glamour and publicity of her debauchery, whose libertine conduct alone led her to share the destiny of the despot who sacrificed the treasures and the blood of his people to his shameful pleasures. You must decide if this Messalina, born among the people, enriched by the cadavers of the people who paid for her moral opprobrium, fallen through the death of the tyrant to the rank where her crime placed her …[96]

This was followed by the description of the execution of the 'woman Du Barry'.

At her execution, Du Barry uttered harrowing cries as she struggled between the executioner and his two assistants, who had great difficulty holding her down. When they tied her to the plank, she implored, 'Mercy, mercy, one more moment, executioner!'[97] Only the blade could silence her. The death of Marie Antoinette, as hideous as it was undeserved, was that of a sovereign and of an abhorrent regime. 'La Du Barry' had come from the people, and her only sin was to have been loved by a king. Fargeon could see her again on her divan, the day she had first received him. With her death, the Revolution had killed his youthful dream, to use his art to bring women to the state of perfect beauty of which Du Barry was the incarnation.

Jean-Louis Fargeon could no longer be called a supporter of the ideals of the Republic. He was now a *ci-devant*, a man of the *ancien régime*. The perfumes being sold in France now had new and terrifying names: *élixirs à la Guillotine* or *Sent-bon à la Sent-son*, in reference to the executioner's last name. A jabot or a handkerchief doused with *essence du lys* or *eau de la Reine* could cost you your life. The 'Capets' perfumer' was completely out of place in the new Parisian market.

He began to look for someone to whom he could sell the business and, to meet with prospective buyers, he had to go to Paris, where he had not set foot in months.[98] The city that had once been the most beautiful and refined in the world was unrecognizable. He passed by a bookshop called Notre Dame de la Guillotine. Celebrations occurred, one after another: the Feast of Virtue, the Feast of Youth, the Feast of Old People. None had anything in common with those of the *ancien régime*. He came across National Guardsmen dressed in the most absurd fashion. Some of them wore hats trimmed in fur, others a horse's mane that fell from the head. One adolescent had on a suit that was half Roman, half Scottish, with bare legs and a tunic with birds' nests in place of epaulettes. A heavy two-edged sword dragged from his imitation tigerskin belt.

The spectacle of the women was scarcely more attractive. Fashion imposed outfits lacking in any grace, *négligés à la patriote* and *toilettes à la Constitution*. The citizen sculptor Especieux wanted to see the French national dress changed to the 'casque and the *khlamys*, as in Athens'. David's student, the citizen artist Wicar, suggested that women abandon the 'ridiculously puffy kerchiefs that concealed their most agreeable charms'. Walls of houses were covered with vicious republican slogans full of mistakes in spelling and syntax. In the streets 'fraternal and patriotic banquets' were held. 'On these Lacedaemonian tables, there is no need for tablecloths, nor napkins, nor of anything resembling luxury,' wrote the *Journal de Paris*. 'In this state of simplicity of the golden age, how many hearts are open to fraternity and sweet equality! Tender fathers and mothers, in the midst of their children, are heartily enjoying the first fruits of the Revolution.' In the streets of the capital, Fargeon had never seen any of this sweet fraternity, just drunkards who stank of sweat, howling insanities. Here, it was intoxication, to the ultimate degree of the dissolute. And, beyond all the outward signs of gaiety, the words of cannibals, and plans of massacre and fire.[99]

The perfumer was more than ever convinced that he had no place in the new France. The Terror grew and raged like a torrent, sweeping away everything in its path. The list of émigrés grew longer every day as they scattered to the four corners of Europe: the Comtesse Béon de Béarn, lady in waiting to Madame Adélaïde, the Marquise and the Duchesse de Choiseul, Mademoiselle Dillon, the Comte and the Comtesse de Duras, the Comtesse de Laage, the Comte Auguste de Lamarck, the Duc and the Duchesse de Luxembourg, the Marquise de Marboeuf, the Vicomtesse de Polastron, the Comte d'Artois, the Marquise de Tonnerre, the Comtesse de Vergennes. All of them had been Fargeon's customers and many of them had neither the time nor the means to pay their debts. Occasionally a scrupulous exile sent back a few pieces of gold with a delicate note of apology for the lateness with which he had made good his debt. In spite of all the outstanding debts, however, Fargeon enjoyed an income of 12,307 livres, which was enough to lead a comfortable life and to continue to pay the obligatory loan for his section of the

National Guard, from which it would have been imprudent, at this time, to resign.[100]

❧ The arrest of the 'Capets' perfumer' ❧

In December 1793, Nivôse of Year II, the House of Fargeon became the firm of Mouchet-Moulinet and Co. The buyers were new men who ran no risk of being taken for friends of the *ci-devants*. Fargeon was immensely relieved no longer to be a merchant. On the occasion of the sale, he had asked the manager of his Nantes branch to come to Paris. With him he brought news of new atrocities. The Revolutionary represent-ative there, Carrier, had inaugurated his reign by drowning eighty priests and, two months later, fifty-eight more. 'What a revolutionary torrent this Loire is!', he had written to the Convention. Trade with foreign countries was suspect, and police surveillance had been reinforced. The proprietors and principal tenants of houses were henceforth obliged to 'post on the outside door, in the most visible place, in legible writing, the names, nicknames, Christian names, ages and professions of all individuals residing within'.[101] In the name of liberty, France was being transformed into an immense prison.

On 8 Nivôse, 4 January 1794 on the old calendar, Fargeon was waiting for a payment coming from abroad in the apart-ment he had kept in the rue du Roule as a pied-à-terre in Paris, when violent blows shook the door. He opened it and a squad of armed members of a section of the militia rushed in. He had dreaded this instant for so long that he was not even surprised. In the past several weeks, many of the former purveyors to the Court had been arrested. The head of the detachment read him the order that he carried:

> The Committee of General Security decrees that the man named Fargeon, residing at 11 rue du Roule, will be seized and brought to a prison, that in his presence his papers will be placed under seal, after examination and extraction of those which will be suspect and whose contents will be reported to

us. We, Citizen Poupard, assisted by Citizens Thomas, Boulanger and Collin, members of the Committee of Surveillance, have been ordered to conduct him to the prison.[102]

Fargeon was accused of doing business with a group of American merchants who had allegedly been caught carrying counterfeit *assignats*. The crime of counterfeiting had always been punished with terrible rigour; a few centuries earlier, those who were found guilty of it were thrown into boiling oil. The Republic followed the example of the monarchy but, wishing to be more humane, it employed the guillotine. Fargeon could not understand how his American correspondents, perfectly honourable men, could have been deceived by counterfeit *assignats*. Asked about his other residence, he produced his very recent passport from the community of Chaumont, dated 29 Frimaire, a card identifying him as an active member of the local section of French guards, and a card of the People's Society. He tried to show that he was a patriot, a friend of liberty, but the militia continued to accuse him of profiting from the vices of the *ci-devant* aristocrats and the hated monarchy. His protestations fell on deaf ears and he was thrown into the Luxembourg prison to await his trial. The day after his arrest, Fargeon declared, 'I was born a man; I loved liberty in 1789 and I have furnished proof to that effect.'[103]

The rue du Roule was searched and two punt guns, a pistol and a few bullets were discovered. On 13 Nivôse, at ten in the morning, Fargeon was taken from prison to explain his possession of the arms that he evidently kept in preparation of an attack against the people. He asserted that he liked to go hunting now and then, but no one believed him. He was then taken to Chaumont, under guard. The house at Chaumont added more fuel to the fire, being too luxurious in the eyes of the Republic for the home of a patriot. The fact that he had bought the house when the Republic put confiscated national properties up for sale made little difference. Citizen Bachot's men put seals on a dozen drawers and pieces of furniture that might contain documents. The following day, the papers were examined in the presence of Citizen Neuville, President of the Committee of Revolutionary Surveillance of the commune of Chaumont.

Fargeon was not allowed to talk to his wife while they were going through his documents. The guard who was supposed to be watching him was a good man and Fargeon knew him well, but they could exchange only a few words. Victoire reassured him that she would try every means to have him released.

There was nothing compromising to be found in the papers, and on 17 Nivôse, at seven in the evening, Fargeon was driven back to Paris and taken again to the Luxembourg prison to be 'placed under guard until his trial'.[104]

❧ Before the Revolutionary Tribunal ❧

The weeks and the months went by, and Fargeon's health deteriorated. He was tormented by gout and he suffered from the after-effects of a fistula operation he had undergone. The perfumer seemed to have been forgotten but he was kept informed of what was going on outside with the continuous arrival of new prisoners. Most of them were there only in passing, and after a brief stay, they would be sent to the scaffold or to another prison. In a few rare cases they were released.

The flood of executions had become uncontrollable and indiscriminate. At the National Convention, Barrère, the president, tried to justify the Terror. 'Only the dead do not speak,' he maintained.[105] In Ventôse, even Jacques René Hébert, the staunch revolutionary, and his entourage were arrested and executed in the space of a month. A few days later, the revolutionary Condorcet committed suicide in his prison cell. Fargeon was dismayed at the news, for he admired him and had read his remarkable *Rapport et projet de décret sur l'organisation générale de l'Instruction publique*. He shared Condorcet's ideals of reason, tolerance and humanity. On 10 Germinal, 30 March according to the old order, a piece of news caused a stir at the prison: Georges Jacques Danton, one of the leaders of the Revolution and the man responsible for the imprisonment of Louis XVI, had just been arrested. He was guillotined in the company of fellow revolutionaries, Camille Desmoulins and Fabre d'Eglantine. In a last demonstration of defiance, Danton asked the executioner to show his head to the people, because 'it was worth the trouble'.[106]

Floréal, which in happier times would have been the merry month of May, produced a frightening crop of heads. On 19 May a batch of twenty-eight former 'farmers general', or tax collectors employed in the service of the old monarchy, were sent to the guillotine. The Tribunal had included Antoine Laurent de Lavoisier in the lot, as he had exercised this financial responsibility as manager of the national tobacco company. Reading the works of the great chemist, Fargeon had been inspired. Lavoisier embodied scientific progress. In his laboratory at Arsenal, the gathering place of all chemists, he had discovered the role of oxygen in combustion and defined the composition of air and of water. He had offered all his knowledge in the service of liberty and had trained the *élèves du salpêtre* so as to arm the nation at war. (Each village trained up volunteers to make saltpetre for use in explosives by the Revolutionary armies.) Lavoisier was in a way 'the Revolution itself against the mindset of the Middle Ages'.[107] He was a patriotic scientist, and the sole excuse given for his murder was the post he had occupied.

⊰⊱

The charges against those tried became increasingly wild. A water carrier by the name of Valentin was condemned to death by the Revolutionary Tribunal of Paris on 28 Prairial as 'accomplice to a plot in Bicêtre jail whose objective was to stab the members of the Committee of Public Security of the Convention, to rip out their hearts, barbecue and eat them, and to punish the most patriotic among them by death in a nail-studded cask'.[108]

At night in his cell Fargeon would start awake, bathed in sweat and consumed with a panicky fear of the blade, but with the light of day he would be filled with a breath of hope. The Terror could not go on like this much longer – it had claimed too many victims. Between 16 Germinal and 22 Prairial, a space of only 430 days, the Revolutionary Tribunal had pronounced 1,251 death sentences. In the two months that followed, 1,376 more unfortunates had been 'shortened'. This was due to the Law of 22 Prairial, also known as the Law of the Reign of Terror, which gave the Revolutionary Tribunal virtually unlimited powers and the accused no rights at all. Even the jailers tired of the frenzied mass slaughter. The people of Paris no longer thronged to see the spectacle of the guillotine, and it had to be removed from the Place de la Revolution and placed at the Barrière du Trône, a less-frequented area, to hide it from sight.

If the nose really lends access to the soul, the Revolution must have had a lowly soul, for it stank of sweat, rotgut wine, urine and blood. Fargeon remembered the scent of Versailles. As he had wandered through stairways and corridors to make his deliveries, he had often found pleasure in the exquisite trail of perfume left by a woman he had just passed. He also thought of Victoire, who moved heaven and earth for him, writing to Robespierre that her husband was well known for his 'republican morality, his consistent aversion to aristocrats, and his constant efforts to seek the company of patriots' and adding that all of his acts were 'marked by civic duty and humanity'.[109]

Eventually, on a day like any other, Fargeon was called to the Tribunal. Four municipal officers were waiting, under the orders of two plumed superintendents who announced themselves as Boulanger and Thomas. The Tribunal was quite close, and they walked across a small courtyard to get there. Fargeon walked into the room that had ironically been re-baptized the 'liberty' chamber after it had become the antechamber to the scaffold. The judges were seated in a row on a platform behind a long table. Fargeon was pushed to a bench

facing them. He was alone, since there were no co-defend-
ants. Behind him, a dozen men and women waited their turn,
their anxiety almost palpable. The president of the Tribunal demanded that Fargeon declare his name and age, then
proceeded to read out the crimes for which the perfumer had
been arrested. He added that since his arrest a witness had
come forward and signed a deposition against him to which
he had to respond. The witness was a man named Dujardin,
the grocer who lived in the street next to Fargeon's.

The president of the Tribunal asked him the first question,
which already sounded like an accusation. He asserted that
Fargeon was purveyor to the last tyrant of France and his
Austrian wife. As such, he had served the cause of the aristocracy rather than that of the people. Fargeon's bankruptcy of
several years earlier was discussed and the accusation of his
spreading counterfeit *assignats* brought up. In reply, Fargeon
pointed out that not one of the Americans arrested for carrying the false bills was ever charged and that one of them
was Thomas Jefferson, plenipotentiary envoy, whose service
to democracy and liberty was widely known and admired
and who could not possibly be a threat to France's fledgling
Republic. In addition, since the release of the Americans, two
other French citizens, arrested on the same charges, had been
released at the request of the People's Societies.

The prosecutor continued his attack, stating that a true
patriot would never possess the trappings of aristocracy that
Fargeon did and that he must, therefore, be as guilty as the
ci-devants he served. His upper-class relatives in Montpellier
were mentioned, as was his ownership of horses, carriages,
several properties and many acres of land – all crimes in the
eyes of the Republic, and punishable by death. Fargeon could
only claim his innocence and reaffirm his devotion to the
Republic and to the ideals for which it stood. He told the court
that he had given 2,400 livres to the Revolution in 1790, as
well as 400 livres in 1792 to his section of the National Guard
to arm and equip a volunteer, and he had promised to donate

300 livres a year as long as the war should continue – a pledge he had fulfilled.

The fact that Fargeon had employed a priest, a 'minister of superstition', as tutor for his children was yet another arrow for the prosecutor's bow, but Fargeon countered by informing him that he had forced the priest to take the oath of the Civil Constitution of the Clergy and had then placed his children's education in the hands of Citizen Carpentier, a declared patriot. The perfumer was also the first in Chaumont to institute the republican calendar, to make his carters work on Sundays and to give them their day off every ten days. He increased their wages by fifteen livres a year to make them less reluctant and raised the wages of his workmen by five livres as an incentive.

The trial continued, with the prosecutor dwelling on Fargeon's wealth and questioning his loyalty to the Republic. Yet every question the prosecutor fired at Fargeon was refuted by the fact that the perfumer had always been, publicly at least, a good and loyal servant of the Republic. The list of things he had done to support the cause appeared endless. In addition to feeding and housing volunteers, he had helped buy three fully trained and equipped horses that the Société Populaire des Sans-culottes of Chaumont, of which he was a member, bought to give to the Republic. Throughout, Fargeon maintained that the money he earned from the *ci-devants* had only enabled him to support the Revolution and the Republic and that the crime of counterfeiting *assignats* could not possibly be carried out by such a patriot.

The court-appointed counsel, whose name Fargeon did not even know, continued in the same vein. He had met with Victoire to organize Fargeon's defence, and she had given him all the evidence of her husband's civic dutifulness that she had been able to gather. His defence began as follows:[110]

Citizens, your inspectors have laboured long months to present to you all that love of the truth, of justice and of impartiality can suggest to republicans who teach a love of the country, knowing no other virtue than that which leads innocence to triumph and crime to the scaffold. And if, as we like to think, Citizen Fargeon has behaved as he has behaved in the community of Chaumont for the past three years, there is no doubt that he will soon be returned to his family and to the country he appears to have sincerely loved. In the research that we have conducted and that we submit to your examination, you will see, citizens, that in the greater part of the facts, some are purely actions of basic humanity, this virtue of sensitive souls. If you do not think you should count them as elements in favour of Fargeon's sense of civic duty, at least your memory may dwell again with tenderness upon the acts of a helping hand, extended more than once to the indigent and the victims of fire, who blessed it. If, on the contrary, you find it fitting to recall them in the act you are called upon to judge, you will acquit the sacred debt of gratitude of our poor and unfortunate compatriots to Fargeon, so that they may one day say, you see, Citizen Fargeon, kindness is never wasted.[111]

Fargeon's life hung in the balance. The president of the court gestured to the guard, who tapped him on the shoulder to indicate that he should leave the dock. The prosecuting jurors and those who would judge retired to deliberate. Finally, a guard led the perfumer back in to hear the verdict. The president repeated the jury's declaration that there was nothing with which he could be charged and that he should be immediately released.

On the very same day, the Republic had just elected to arrest Robespierre. They had also beheaded the Comtesse d'Ossun, who had been arrested in her house in the rue de Varenne and accused of having participated in the conspiracies of the corrupt monarchy. It was said that she went to her death with all the courage and serenity of a martyr.

News of the arrest and condemnation of Robespierre had arrived in Chaumont before Fargeon, and people were dancing in the streets that were lit with torches to celebrate the end of the Terror. Perhaps the perfumer felt a surge of renewed hope. After so much bloodshed, France might finally know the blessings of the Republic of the Rights of Man.

Epilogue

Once he had escaped the guillotine, Marie Antoinette's perfumer had but one ambition, to retire comfortably and finish his days in peace. But that was not to be. After a while, he returned to his boutique in the rue du Roule that the new owners, having neither his experience nor his reputation, had brought to ruin. Under the Directoire of the new constitution, Fargeon perfumed the *Incroyables*, the *Muscadins* and the *Merveilleuses*. Under the Empire, he became the 'Perfumer-distiller approved as purveyor to the Empress'. But his health had been permanently damaged by his days in prison, and he died aged fifty-eight, in his apartment in the rue du Roule, on 9 November 1806.

His widow and his sons created a company to continue the business, which became Fargeon frères after Victoire's death, but it was dissolved on 17 July 1815. Auguste-Frédéric took over the boutique in the rue du Roule while Antoine-Louis set up a store called Fargeon Jeune at 13, rue Vivienne. They amicably shared the equipment and the clientele and they worked together to exploit the family recipes and formulae to their greatest advantage. When the rue de Rivoli was built through, Antoine-Louis had to transfer his boutique to 319, rue Saint-Honoré, where it remained until 1830. Auguste-Frédéric became perfumer to the King and the 'new Court', including the Duchesse de Berry. In 1824 he sold his business to Jean Baptiste Gellé. The House of Gellé frères upheld its reputation for its 'scientifically produced products' until the eve of the First World War. Its factory was located in Neuilly, near the Porte Maillot. Destroyed by Prussian bombs in 1870, it was rebuilt in Levallois, not far from the Oriza perfume shop that had been founded by the cousin who had recommended Jean-Louis Fargeon to Madame Vigier.

Among the Queen's purveyors who had escaped the guillotine, Rose Bertin retired to her home in Epinay, where she died in 1813. The sprightly coiffeur Léonard – whose brother had been executed with Chénier – was able to emigrate and lived in Germany and in Moscow for a while before returning to France with Louis XVIII. He never rebuilt his fortune and died in 1820. The property of Suresnes that Jean-Louis Fargeon acquired in 1786 bordered the Château de la Source, which belonged to the Comte de Skelton. A century and a half later, the famous perfumer François Coty made it his home, installing his Cité des Parfums there in 1904.

Appendices

APPENDIX 1

The Palette of Jean-Louis Fargeon

Extracted from Jean-Louis Fargeon, *L'Art du parfumeur*, Paris, 1801.

I list here the plant and animal species from which we drew the basic preparations we used as well as those that enter into the complex composition of products we made in the province of Languedoc and the region of Grasse. However, the dividing line between the attributions of apothecaries and perfumers was not yet clearly established. I also include the ingredients of preparations such as *eau d'Arquebusade, eau vulnéraire* or *eau de Mélisse* as well as certain vinegars that have antiseptic qualities. These different species enter into the creation of plain or composite *eaux*, according to the particular vision of each artist.

Incense or **olibanum** comes from Arabia. It is a pale yellow, transparent, resinous substance. Beads of it look like mastic, but are larger. Incense is dry and hard, with a slightly bitter taste, moderately acrid and resinous, not unpleasant, with a penetrating odour. Drops of incense are transparent, oblong and smooth. They look like testicles or breasts, hence the names male and female incense. This perfume is used to spread a pleasant odour in the temples of nearly every religion. Incense from the Indies and from Moka arrives in Europe on East India Company ships, sometimes in the form of small drops, but usually in mass quantities.

Myrrh is a fragrant gum resin that comes from India in the form of yellow or red, slightly transparent beads or chunks. It has a bitter taste, a bit pungent and aromatic, that causes nausea. If crushed or burned, it exudes a rather unpleasant odour. It should be oily and crumbly. The pieces that are very transparent and not bitter inside are just gum arabic. Those that are brownish, viscous and disagreeable-smelling should be rejected as well.

Benzoin is a hard, fragile, dry, inflammable resin. It gives off a sweet and penetrating odour when burned, with a fragrance of vanilla. It is drained from an incision in a great tree called the *belzof*, which grows on Sumatra and on Java, or in the kingdom of Siam. If this resin is drawn at the ideal time, it is beautiful and brilliant, but if it remains in the tree too long, it becomes brown and polluted with waste. Benzoin is sublimated into silver flowers when held over a flame in a retort surrounded by sand and covered with a paper cone. These flowers are used in perfumes. The plain resin, dissolved in spirits of wine, yields a dye, a few drops of which make the *eau* to which they are added milky and cloudy. This is what is termed virginal milk. Ladies use it as a grooming cosmetic.

Styrax or **storax calamite** is a resin taken from incisions in the trunk or in the branches of a tree known as the *alibousier*, whose flowers resemble those of the orange tree and which grows in the forests of Provence, of Syria and of Cilicia. Storax calamite resin is greyish, shiny, fairly dense, and has a rather pungent but agreeable flavour and an odour of Balm of Peru, very lush and very penetrating. The attribute 'calamite' comes from the fact that long ago, it was shipped from Pamphilia to Marseilles, enveloped in reeds. An American variety of styrax also exists, a balm obtained with or without incising the tree, from the bark of a tree found in Louisiana, believed to be the Virginia sycamore or plane tree. This resinous sap has the consistency of an oily varnish and is reddish yellow, with an aromatic, acrid flavour and an odour that is close to that of styrax or of ambergris.

Ladanum is a resinous substance gathered from the Cistus bush that grows in Cyprus, in Candia, in Greece and in Italy. Perfumers make it into a fragrant oil that is an ingredient in the composition of tablets.

Galbanum is an oily substance, as ductile as wax, semi-transparent and shiny. The galbanum plant, which Dioscorides called *metopion*, grows in Arabia, in Syria, in Persia and in many African countries, particularly Mauritania.

Balm of Mecca is a yellowish-white liquid resin with an acrid and aromatic flavour something like that of the lemon. It is obtained by cutting into a bush called the veritable balm, which grows wild in upper Arabia, Judaea and Egypt. The species is very rare here. Ladies who use this balm as a cosmetic make it into a virginal milk and a 'sultana's cream', both of which are considered very effective beauty treatments for the skin.

Musk comes from the East Indies and also from Tonkin [Indochina]. It comes from an animal that seems to be a species of gazelle or, rather, roebuck, which carries the musk in a tiny pouch near the umbilicus. The purest musk, most prized by the Chinese, is that which the animal leaves as a trail on stones or on tree trunks he rubs against. It is often subject to adulteration or substitution. Musk that comes without its envelope should be dry, with a very strong odour, tan coloured and bitter to taste. It should leave no residue when burned. The envelope containing the musk should be covered with the brown hairs of the animal's skin. If the hairs are white, that is a sign that it is Bengal musk, inferior in quality to musk from Tonkin.

The fragrant liquid we call **civet** comes from the pouch or sac beneath the anus of the animal of the same name, found in

Africa, which is termed a beaver in the Guinean language. This liquid is a secretion that has a creamy or honey-like consistency and is white. As it ages, it yellows and darkens. Its odour, though strong, is never disagreeable and is sweeter than that of musk.

Ambergris is found on the seashore, in more or less large pieces. It is a light, opaque substance, ash-coloured, sprinkled with small, white spots that give off an odour which becomes much more pronounced when added to a small amount of other aromatic substances. Ambergris by itself exudes an earthy odour, but when it is added to mixtures, it lends an 'ethereal delicacy to perfumes'. Ambergris of good quality burns easily, leaving a golden-coloured liquid resin. Perfumers use it extensively and heighten its appeal to the sense of smell by mixing it with a small amount of musk, civet or sugar. Yellow amber, a hard, bituminous substance with a slightly bitter taste, is found on the Prussian coast, on the Baltic Sea.

Ambrette is a seed about the size of a millet grain whose scent resembles that of musk. It comes from the fruit of a plant common to Galam country [Senegal], the Antilles, Arabia and Egypt.

Sweet-smelling costus is an exotic root taken from a shrub a good deal like the elder tree that grows in upper Arabia, Malabar, Brazil and Surinam. It is cut in thumb-sized, oblong pieces and has a faint odour of violet. In antiquity, it was used to make seasonings and perfumes and it was burned on the altar like incense.

The **calamus** or aromatic reed, found in Egypt or the Indies, is used in the composition of certain perfumes. It is the stem of a plant that is hollow like a drinking straw, about as thick as a mediocre quill pen, and full of a spongy or soft substance that has an acrid flavour and a rather pleasing odour.

Other perfumes are taken from flowers or from wood. The flowers are those common in the zone that extends from the Mediterranean coast up to Grasse. Here is a list:

Aloe is the wood of a tree that grows in Indochina, of which we can distinguish three species. The first is the Indian calambac, or tambac, a resinous wood that reacts to pressure rather like wax. It melts like resin when placed on a fire and exudes a sweet odour. This wood is much prized by the nobles of China and Japan and is worth its weight in gold there. The Chinese burn it in their temples. When they wish to receive someone in great splendour, with a sumptuous celebration, they put this wood in earthenware dishes, and its pleasant odour permeates the rooms. This wood is so prized and precious in China that it is hard to come by here. The second species is the one we find in boutiques. It comes from the East in pieces of different sizes and is heavy, reddish brown with black and resinous lines here and there, and full of tiny holes that contain a fragrant reddish resin. Placed on hot coals, this wood releases a rather pleasant odour. The third kind of aloe wood is eagle wood, which comes from Mexico.

The **béen** [an ancient resin] is the fruit of a tree native to Egypt. It is much prized by perfumers, and the oil extracted from it is excellent for the correction of skin flaws. It actively conserves the scent of flowers without in any way altering it, since it has no fragrance of its own, and it almost never becomes rancid. The flowers are placed in layers upon a horsehair sieve, and a piece of cotton which has been soaked in béen oil is then placed upon the flowers. The oil then takes in the predominating emanation of the flowers that is responsible for their odour. The same cotton can be placed on several lots of flowers. Then the oil is pressed from it. The result is the essential oil of the flowers.

The Orientals loved **sandalwood**, whose sawdust was an ingredient of the recipe for incense and whose essence formed the basis for all of their perfumes. The most sought-after was citrin-coloured sandalwood, 'whose odour is sweet but a bit too cloying for European tastes; its principal positive quality is its great tenacity'.

South American **rosewood, Rhodes wood** from the Orient, and North American **sassafras** all have a refreshing odour that is perfect for soaps.

Bergamot is a type of orange. Its bark is used to make boxes for sweets, and one can extract an essential oil and an *esprit ardent* that are particularly sharp. In the citrus family, I am also fond of sweet orange, bitter orange, lemon, citron and limette. The essence of citron is extracted from the fruits of the *citrus medica* and is very often used in eau de Cologne. Limette is an essence that comes from the fruit of the *citrus aurantifolia* and is obtained either through cold pressing or distillation by steam. The orchards are located in Provence and in Italy.

The **bitter orange** or **bigaradier** is virtually a goldmine for those who grow it, because every part of the tree gives off its perfume. This tree, which originated in India, covers the hills of Grasse and its environs. The flowers provide *eau distillée* or *eau de fleur d'oranger*, essence or *néroli*, oil or pomade. The leaves give *essence de petit grain*. The fruits give *essence de bigarade*, which is used in the fabrication of eau de Cologne. *Essence* or *essence de Portugal* can be obtained from the sweet orange tree. The blossom season begins around mid-April and runs through to May and June.

Jasmine, one of the jewels among the products of Grasse, was imported to Europe by the Arabs in 1629. The *jasminum grandiflorum* demanded a special treatment before it could be grown in this region. It was done by first grafting a wild variety that flowered during the first year. The bushes are three or four feet high and must be planted at airy heights but protected nonetheless from the wind. The blossom appears

from July to October. The flowers open at six in the evening
and must be picked immediately on short days, or the following morning after the dew has evaporated. A single night of
frost can wipe out everything. This delicate work of cultiva-
tion and harvesting has become a speciality of Grasse, and
the jasmine of Grasse is one of the finest owing to the skill of
the labourers. The fragrance of jasmine flowers is so delicious
that various fluids have been used to attempt to carry it. (Its
flowers do not render the scented liquid necessary for distillation.) The essence of jasmine that comes from Italy is only
béen oil scented with jasmine blossom. For this effect, cotton
is soaked in béen oil, and the pieces of cotton are arranged by
layers, with layers of jasmine flowers placed between them.
The cotton soaks up the odour, and the very strong-smelling
oil is then expressed from the cotton. The fragrance can be
conserved for some time, provided the bottle in which it is
stored is tightly corked. To transfer this odour of jasmine to
esprit de vin, which cannot be done even by distillation, the
oil of the *esprit de vin* must be poured on the scented oil of
béen, and the mixture then shaken well. The odour of jasmine
completely abandons the oily substance and transfers to the
esprit de vin; the drawback, however, is that the latter permits
the odour to escape very easily.

The **jonquil** gives off a very pleasant smell; nonetheless not
everyone finds it attractive.

The **iris** is widely used to give a fragrance of violet to
perfumes. This flower is cultivated all over Europe, but the
best ones are those grown in Florence, in Tuscany. When dry,
it has a distinct scent of violet, but it loses this in contact with
alcohol, which dissolves the resinous part of the flower. When
the rhizomes of the iris are appropriately treated, the result
is products of great delicacy that can be used in many different floral compositions. Along with the rose, the iris rhizome
is one of the most ancient raw materials of floral odour. It is
used in all of the perfumery 'à la violette' which is so popular.

Other roots that are part of the perfumer's art: **angelica**, the root of which provides an excellent infusion, and **vetiver**, or *anatherum muriaticum* root, which is grown in the Indies.

Lavender flowers are distilled with white wine, *eau de vie*, or *esprit de vin*. The perfumer uses the latter to produce *esprit de lavande*, which has several uses, including perfuming the water one washes in. Its essential oil, freshly distilled and well rectified, can be mixed with a good *esprit de vin*. Lavender has always been appreciated as an element of the perfumer's palette for its refreshing and tonic odour. The Romans used it in their baths. Lavender is grown in the south of France, but the heat of the climate there makes it slightly acrid. Lavender grown in England is of exceptionally fine quality.

The fragrant water extracted from the **lily** or **lis** blossom through a *bain-marie* process was once used to heighten the colour of young ladies. It removed any blotches on the face, especially if mixed with a bit of salts of tartar.

Myrtle flowers, when distilled in water, produce an astringent lotion called *eau d'ange*. It is known for its pleasant odour and often used for bathing. It is the very best product for perfuming and cleansing and for stimulating the skin to improve its firmness.

The **rose** is an essential raw material in the production of perfumery. It can be used to make *eau distillée*, essence and oil, as well as pomades and sachets. Nine-tenths of rose essence comes from the Balkans, near Kizanlick. This essence, in its pure state, remains crystallized at high temperatures, but it was common in countries producing it to doctor it by adding essence of geranium and spermaceti to give it a false appearance of crystallization. Consequently, perfumers much preferred the **rose of Provence** or **May rose**, the *rosa centifolia*. It blooms in the month of May and women and children must pick the flowers at daybreak, for if they are picked in the heat of the day, they lose all their sweetness.

The **tuberose** is indigenous to the Indies. It also grows wild on the island of Java and in Ceylon. It was brought to Europe in 1594 by Simon de Torar, a Spanish doctor. The bulb is planted in the autumn and blooms the following year. It is replanted every year. The flower begins to bloom in June and July and continues until early September. The stem is a metre long, and every day two flowers open up from eleven in the morning until three in the afternoon. They must be picked immediately, otherwise their ephemeral fragrance is difficult to control. These bulbous flowers produce an essence that is a capital element for the perfumer's palette.

The **cassier**, or **cassia**, of the acacia family, is cultivated from October to November. Its tingling and penetrating perfume affords a refreshing note useful to the perfumer. It resembles in some ways the scent of the violet, and it is used to reinforce the weak fragrance of this flower.

The **violet** has a fine and sweet odour whose popularity is increasing. It cannot be distilled, but it can be collected through the use of essential oils. It is planted in Nice and in the surrounding countryside, beneath orange and lemon trees whose thick foliage protects it from the harshness of the sun.

Rosemary provides a very strong essence that is used to perfume ordinary soap. This odour is very close to that of camphor, used for marriages and funerals and the principal ingredient of *eau de la Reine de Hongrie*.

Thyme, **wild thyme**, **marjoram**, **basil flower**, **celery**, **parsley**, **laurel**, **absinth**, **fennel**, and **sage** all provide essences. **Mint**, like thyme, blossoms in the month of June and must be picked in hot, dry weather. The leaves and the flowers should be stripped from the stem, two pounds of them crushed and immediately placed in the still. The liquid collected has a taste and a smell that are both strong and pleasant, and that is why it should be used very sparingly.

Spices serve the purpose of emphasizing the weak sweetness of a plant. **Cinnamon, cloves, mace, nutmeg, cardamom, coriander** and others are wonderful aromatics to use as a support to perfect the perfumer's creation. Cinnamon is distilled from the bark of two species of laurel that flourish in India and in China. The clove is the bud of the flower of *caryophyllus aromaticus*, which comes from the coast of Africa and from the Indian Archipelago. Its essence is used in soap and, in moderate dosage, in the composition of a few perfumes, such as that of the carnation, with which it has an affinity. Mace and nutmeg are products of the same tree, *myristica moschata*, which grows in the Indies. One is the fibrous envelope of the fruit, and the other is the fruit itself. **Allspice** or **pimento** is the berry of the *Eugénia pimenta* that grows in the tropics, particularly in the Antilles. Two kinds of star anise or badian come from China.

Ambrette comes from South America. **Anise, dill, fennel** and **caraway** are found in Europe.

APPENDIX 2

Procedures for the Manufacture of Perfumes

Extracted from Jean-Louis Fargeon, *L'Art du parfumeur*, Paris, 1801; Diderot and d'Alembert, *Encyclopédie*, Paris, 1754; Jacques Savary des Brulons, *Dictionnaire universel du commerce*, 1762.

❧ a. Distillation and vessels for distillation ❧

The only instrument necessary for distillation is the still, a vessel of tin-plated copper, pewter or glass, the latter being 'the most conducive to the purity of spirituous substances'. The still is composed of three distinct pieces: the boiler or retort, the head and the cooler.

The **boiler** is a sort of a cauldron whose shape is like a truncated cone that is turned upside down. It is driven into a brick stove until its exterior surface is supported by a shelf resting on the stove. It should be as deep as its diameter is wide. The bottom is normally round and concave, which provides the greatest surface of contact for the fire. This boiler, well coated with tin, also has a neck, which shortens the opening slightly. The neck is equipped with a mouth that has two handles.

The head or cover of the boiler is of tin-plated copper in the large vessels and of thin pewter in the small ones. Its shape is that of a cylinder that ends in a segment of a sphere. In the lower part of the cylinder, it has a neck that fits tightly into the opening of the boiler.

The final cap is soldered a little beneath the upper edge of the cylinder. At the centre of this cap is a mouth. A large, slightly conical pipe, called the *bec du chapiteau*, is soldered to the side of the cylinder.

The substances to be distilled are placed in the boiler, the cover placed on it and fixed tightly, and it is closed. The fire is then made in the stove. Then, through the action of the heat, the substances are transformed into steam in the cover and evacuated through the extremity of the *bec* to arrive in the third piece, where they condense upon cooling. That is why this part is called the **condenser** or **cooler**. Initially it was equipped with a long piece of tubing, but that took up too much space, and with a spiral (the condenser was then termed a coil), but this was difficult to clean after distillation of the aromatic matter. It finally adopted a zigzag shape, which is at least as efficient and much easier to clean.

The *bain-marie* or **double-boiler** is an essential piece of equipment for the perfumer, because it can be used to distil very volatile substances, or those that can only stand a degree of heat below that of boiling water. It consists of a cylindrical pewter vessel to contain the retort, which fits snugly in the opening of the boiler and rests upon the collar, so that its bottom does not touch the bottom of the boiler. Thus, the distillation can be done either with or without the *bain-marie*.

In this method of distillation, the vessel is filled with the chosen substances and placed in the boiler, then covered with the head. Water is then poured through the mouth into the boiler. The upper part of the boiler being hollow on the outside, this space is filled with crushed charcoal, which does not conduct heat, so as to prevent the steam from condensing in this part and settling in the retort. 'When the operation calls for a stronger fire, a *bain de sable* [literally, a sand bath] can be used. This is an iron cauldron capable of resisting fire, which is filled with fine sand in which the still is placed, so that the sand is a good finger's breadth higher than the level of the matter contained in the retort. This *bain* is sensitive to nearly all degrees of heat, from the most moderate right up to incandescence, and for this reason it is very useful. It can be an adequate method for most operations, in fact, if the artist has acquired enough experience to handle it properly.'

The perfumer also uses the process of **rectification** to obtain very pure and very sweet liquids for perfumes. To rectify is to put already distilled liquids through the distillation process once again. To accomplish this, the perfumer uses both the *bain-marie* and the *bain de sable*, with stills made of glass.

When they have a large enough capacity, the glass retorts are equipped with a pipe located on the upper part of the dome, so that they can be easily filled on the spot. The liquids can be entered either all at once, using a funnel, or separately, using an S-shaped tube, adapted to the pipe, which also serves as a safety tube.

Sometimes an extension or *allonge* is added to the retort. This is a double-necked vessel, bulging in the middle, which serves to make the neck of the retort longer.

The perfumer also needs *matras*, or small glass flagons, either with long necks or with curved necks and tubing.

And finally, the perfumer also uses a filter. This consists of a piece of metallic fabric that is either tin-plated, galvanized, silver-plated or silver, folded like a filter. It has a number of folds equal to that of the paper filter it is designed to hold and support. The surface of the paper is applied to the metallic fabric and, since it is neither obstructed nor affected by any adherence, the liquid can pass freely, allowing the whole process to proceed with a rapidity that depends only upon the state of this liquid. The conical shape of this accelerating filter is such that it can be placed in funnels of glass or of another substance. The filter can be cleaned easily by shaking it in water and drying it over heat.

❧ b. Enfleurage, or maceration ❧

In this process, the perfumer uses a box entirely lined in tin plate, so that the edge does not transmit any odour of flowers whatsoever or absorb any of the essence. Wooden frames are made to easily fit flat into the box. Their slats should be two fingers thick and edged all round with the points of needles. A piece of cotton fabric should be stretched over each frame. Before use, the material should be thoroughly washed, rinsed in clean water and dried.

Once the cotton pieces have been soaked in oil of béen, the perfumer presses out some of the liquid and then stretches them over the frames, attaching them to the needles. Then he places a frame at the bottom of the box, with the fabric side up. Next he scatters in the flowers whose essence he wants to capture, covering them with another frame on whose fabric he places another layer of flowers, continuing the process until the box is full. Since the wood is two fingers thick, the flowers are never pressed. Twelve hours later, the perfumer can place other flowers there, even continuing the process over several days. This process is called *enfleurage*.

When the scent seems strong enough to him, he removes the pieces of fabric from the frames and folds them in four. Then, after folding and rolling them up, tying them with a string to hold them and prevent their stretching too much, he puts them in the press, to squeeze out the oil. This press should also be of tin plate, so that the wood does not absorb any oil.

[The perfumer] gathers the essence in meticulously clean receptacles placed beneath the press and then transfers it to tightly sealed flasks. He can only extract the essence of one flower at a time in a box, because the odour of one would spoil the other, and, for the same reason, cotton cloths that have served to capture the essence of one flower cannot be used for another, unless they have been thoroughly washed in clean water and dried. This is the usual method for obtaining the odour of flowers that do not exude essential oils when they are distilled, such as tuberose, jasmine and many others. This is a very useful process in the art of perfumery, but it is also very slow, since it requires thirty to thirty-five days to obtain a satisfactory result, during which time the flowers must be renewed each day, leaving the same grease spread on the glass. This technique demands skilled labour, usually feminine. The flowers must be treated within twenty-four hours.

❧ c. Expression ☙

Pressing or **expression** is only used for orange, lemon and citron peels; thus it is used exclusively to extract citrus essence (from oranges, lemons, bergamot and citron). There are several local traditional methods. In Genoa, the fruits are rubbed against a funnel with holes in it. In Sicily, the peel is cut in very fine pieces and pressed in cloth bags. In Calabra, where production is most developed, the fruits are placed between two bowls superimposed on one another and covered with small points. Above is the convex part, below the concave. The perfumer turns the two bowls in opposite directions, and when the vesicles are pierced, he takes out the fruits and wipes them off with a sponge. The result is an essence of zest, prized for its delicacy. The perfumer can also obtain an essence of zest through distillation, although it is inferior in quality.

Notes

1. Municipal Archives of Montpellier.
2. Simon Barbe, *Le Parfumeur François*, Lyon, 1693.
3. Antoine Dejean, *Traité de la distillation avec un Traité des odeurs*, Paris, 1753, and *Traité des odeurs, Suite du Traité de la distillation*, Paris, 1764.
4. L. Domaison, Montpellier in 1760 according to *Voyages en Languedoc*, volume IV, Archives of the town of Montpellier, inventories and documents.
5. Bankruptcy files: Statements and balance sheet, 1716–1780. Hérault Departmental Archives.
6. Cf. Béatrice Rivet, *La Parfumerie ancienne à Montpellier, xvie–xviiie siècle*, Municipal Library of Montpellier.
7. *Encyclopédie ou Dictionnaire raisonné des sciences, des arts et des métiers*, published by MM. Diderot and d'Alembert, Briasson, Paris, 1754, vol IV, pp 1053–4, vol XXV, pp 1048–9.
8. Declaration, 20 September 1743, II E 56/523. Marquès, notary ADH. Fargeon/Salles Marriage: Act of 20 January 1744. Municipal Archives of Montpellier.
9. *Encyclopédie*, Diderot and D'Alembert, vol IV, pp 1053–4, vol XXV, pp 1048–9.
10. E.B. de Condillac, *Traité des sensations*, in *Œuvres philosophiques*, republished Paris: PUF, 1947, p 222.
11. Denis Diderot, *Lettres sur les sourds et les muets*.

12. Jacques Savary des Brulons, *Dictionnaire universel du commerce, d'histoire naturelle, des arts et métiers*, 1762.

13. Jean-Jacques Rousseau, *L'Emile, projet d'éducation idéale*, 1762.

14. Comtesse d'Adhémar, *Souvenirs sur Marie-Antoinette et sur la Cour de Versailles*, Paris, 1836.

15. Marquise de Durfort, cited in Pierre de Nolhac, *Autour de la reine*, Tallandier, 1929, p 16.

16. Germain Brice, *Description nouvelle de la ville de Paris*, Paris, 1698, 1706, 1725.

17. *Mémoires du comte Alexandre de Tilly*, Paris, 1929.

18. Cited in A. Cabanes, *Mœurs intimes du passé*, Geneva: Farnot, 1976, vol. 1, p 254.

19. Comtesse d'Adhémar, *Souvenirs sur Marie-Antoinette et sur la Cour de Versailles*.

20. Sapphires was a contemporary name for pimples.

21. Marquis de Bouillé, cited in Pierre de Nolhac, *Autour de la reine*.

22. Jean-Louis Fargeon, *L'Art du parfumeur ou traité complet de la préparation des parfums, cosmétiques, pommades, pastilles, odeurs, huiles antiques, essences, bains aromatiques et gants de senteur*, Paris, 1801.

23. *Ibid.*, p 109.

24. *Ibid.*, pp 202–9.

25. Comtesse d'Adhémar, *Souvenirs sur Marie-Antoinette et sur la Cour de Versailles*.

26. Guy Chaussinand-Nogaret, *La Vie quotidienne des femmes du roi*, Paris: Hachette, 1990, p 239.

27. *Correspondance entre Marie-Antoinette et Marie-Thérèse*, Paris, 1933.

28. AN (Archives Nationales): Notaries' minute book, étude XLVII, marriage contract Ravoisié/Fargeon, 26 July 1774.

29. Bibliothèque de la Ville de Paris, Current Events Series 120, Houbigant file.

30. Fargeon, *L'Art du parfumeur*.

31. Article, 'Rouge', in the *Encyclopédie*.

32. Fargeon, *L'Art du parfumeur.*

33. *Mémoires du comte Alexandre de Tilly.*

34. Comtesse d'Adhémar, *Souvenirs sur Marie-Antoinette et sur la Cour de Versailles.*

35. *Correspondance entre Marie-Antoinette et Marie-Thérèse.*

36. *Ibid.*

37. Pierre, Victor, Baron de Besenval, *Mémoires du Baron de Bésenval sur la Cour de France,* republished Paris, 1987.

38. Comtesse d'Adhémar, *Souvenirs sur Marie-Antoinette et sur la Cour de Versailles,* pp 113–14.

39. Cited in Pierre de Nolhac, *Autour de la reine.*

40. Cited in Bordonove, *Les Bourbons: de Louis XVI à Louis-Philippe, 1774–1848,* 2004.

41. Madame Campan, *Mémoires de Madame Campan, première femme de chambre, sur la vie privée de Marie-Antoinette,* republished Paris, 1988, p 901.

42. Fargeon, *L'Art du parfumeur,* pp 385–6.

43. *Ibid.*

44. *Ibid.*

45. Comtesse d'Adhémar, *Souvenirs sur Marie-Antoinette et sur la Cour de Versailles,* p 179.

46. *Ibid.*

47. Fargeon, *L'Art du parfumeur.*

48. Comtesse d'Adhémar, *Souvenirs sur Marie-Antoinette et sur la Cour de Versailles.*

49. Baronne d'Oberkirch, *Mémoires sur la Cour de Louis XVI et la Société Française avant 1789,* Paris, 1970, anecdotes from Spring 1782.

50. Madame Campan, *Mémoires de Madame Campan.*

51. Comtesse d'Adhémar, *Souvenirs sur Marie-Antoinette et sur la Cour de Versailles.*

52. AN AP61: *Mémoires de J.-L. Fargeon à Monsieur Frère du Roy de 1780 à 1786.* Monsieur Dimanche is a character from Molière's *Dom Juan* who would never pay his debts.

53. Charles-Félix, Comte de France d'Hézecques, Memoirs of a page in the Court of Louis XVI, cited in Pierre de Nolhac, *Autour de la reine*, p 240.

54. Archives de Paris (AP) D4B6, carton 70, dossier 4589: Bankruptcy of Jean-Louis Fargeon, 4 January 1779.

55. Letter of Marie Antoinette, 12 June 1778.

56. AP D4B6, carton 70, dossier 4589: Bankruptcy of Jean-Louis Fargeon, 4 January 1779, greffe 2235.

57. Madame Campan, *Mémoires de Madame Campan*.

58. Madame Vigée-Lebrun, *Souvenirs*, vol 1, letter 5.

59. Fargeon, *L'Art du parfumeur*, p 201.

60. Madame Vigée-Lebrun, *Souvenirs*, vol 1, letter 5.

61. *Mémoires du comte Alexandre de Tilly*, pp 14–15.

62. Madame Vigée-Lebrun, *Souvenirs*.

63. L.A. Caraccioli, *La Critique des dames et des messieurs à leur toilette*, Paris, 1770.

64. AN Series 01: House of the Queen: Statement of Expenditures of Wardrobe of the Queen 1782–1785.

65. Madame d'Ossun: General State of the Expenditure of the Wardrobe of the Queen, 1782.

66. Stefan Zweig, *Marie-Antoinette*, 1937.

67. Cited in Bordonove, *Les Bourbons*.

68. Madame Vigée-Lebrun, *Souvenirs*.

69. Madame Campan, *Mémoires de Madame Campan*.

70. Cf. Emile Langlade, *La Marchande des modes de Marie-Antoinette, Rose Bertin*, Paris: Albin Michel, 1911.

71. Madame Vigée-Lebrun, *Souvenirs*, vol 1, p 37.

72. AN MC and VII/472: Sale of the house and garden at Suresnes, 31 January 1786.

73. Fargeon, *L'Art du parfumeur*, pp 42, 84.

74. *Ibid.*, p 2.

75. Comtesse d'Adhémar, *Souvenirs sur Marie-Antoinette et sur la Cour de Versailles*, p 25.

76. Jean-Léonard Autié, *Souvenirs de Léonard, coiffeur de la Reine Marie-Antoinette*, Paris: A. Fayard, 1905.

77. Fargeon, *L'Art du parfumeur*, p 93.

78. Madame Campan, *Mémoires de Madame Campan*, book II, chapter 1.

79. Michelet, *La Révolution Française*, Laffont Bouquins.

80. Madame Campan, *Mémoires de Madame Campan*, book II, chapter 18.

81. Description of the inventory of the toilet kit of Marie Antoinette, Musée du Louvre, Paris.

82. Madame Campan, *Mémoires de Madame Campan*.

83. *Ibid.*

84. Comtesse d'Adhémar, *Souvenirs sur Marie-Antoinette et sur la Cour de Versailles*.

85. Madame Campan, *Mémoires de Madame Campan*.

86. Michelet, *La Révolution Française*.

87. AN KK 378: 1792, supplies of M. Fargeon to the Temple. AN 01 3799: Supplies of June 1792 of M. Fargeon, master-perfumer in Paris.

88. Emile Langlade, *La Marchande des modes de Marie-Antoinette, Rose Bertin*.

89. Soulavie, *Mémoires historiques et politiques du règne de Louis XVI*, vol 6.

90. Michelet, *La Révolution Française*.

91. Jean-Baptiste Hanet, known as Cléry, *Journal de ce qui s'est passé à la tour du Temple pendant la captivité de Louis XVI, roi de France, et autres mémoires sur le Temple*, edited by Jacques Brosse, Paris: Mercure de France, 1968.

92. Prudhomme, *Révolution de Paris n°161, journal logographique, première législature supplément au Tome XXVI*.

93. Cléry, *Journal de ce qui s'est passé à la tour du Temple pendant la captivité de Louis XVI*.

94. AN F7 4391: signed original and AN 01 3799: Supplies of June 1792 from M. Fargeon, master-perfumer in Paris.

95. From the memoirs of Rosalie Lamorlière.

96. Michelet, *La Révolution Française*.

97. *Ibid.*

98. AN F7 4391: Supplies of perfumery made by M. Fargeon, perfumer for the service of the Children of France, regulated on 4 March 1793.

99.   Testimony of Convention member Edme Monnet cited by André Castelot, in *Historama*, July 1974.

100.   AN F7 4702: Arrest and judgement of Jean-Louis Fargeon, Committee of Surveillance.

101.   Michelet, *La Révolution Française*.

102.   AN F7 4702: Arrest and judgement of Jean-Louis Fargeon, Committee of Surveillance.

103.   AN F7 4702: Declaration of honour, signed by J.-L. Fargeon.

104.   AN F7 4702, no 757: Section of the French Guards, 6 and 17 Nivôse, Year II.

105.   Michelet, *La Révolution Française*.

106.   *Ibid.*

107.   The expression comes from Michelet.

108.   Alphabetical list of those guillotined during the Revolution, http://les.guillotines.free.fr

109.   AN F7 4702: Arrest and judgement of Jean-Louis Fargeon, Committee of Surveillance.

110.   AN F7 4702: part no 33.

111.   *Ibid.*